apexart

Life Between Borders:
The Nomadic Life of Curators and Artists

Life Between Borders: The Nomadic Life of Curators and Artists
Edited by Steven Rand and Heather Felty
ISBN: 978-1-933347-65-3
1. Cultural Studies 2. Sociology 3. Art History
4. Anthropology 5. Art 6. Globalization

apexart
291 Church Street
New York, NY 10013
t: 212 431 5270
www.apexart.org
info@apexart.org

Contents

apexart is a 501(c)(3) nonprofit visual arts organization founded in 1994 by artist Steven Rand. Originally an exhibition venue, it's activities now also include an international residency program, book publishing, an active public program, and occasional conferences.

Life Between Borders: The Nomadic Life of Curators and Artists is the fourth book in the apexart series which consider issues in the visual arts. The first book, *On Cultural Influence*, published in 2006, is a collection of essays from past conferences in Poland, Brazil, and Hawaii. *Cautionary Tales: Critical Curating*, published in 2007, addressed the changing role of the contemporary curator. *Playing by the Rules: Alternative Thinking/Alternative Spaces*, published in 2010, considered the responsibility of alternative spaces today.

Special thanks to Niels Van Tomme, who served as project advisor, and NLW for continued support in many ways.

Steven Rand

Forward

I'm in Artistan, a smallish city with a great café that I'm sitting in now. There are several galleries, a museum, and a small arts community. The openings I attended were very nice and the dinner after the museum opening was in a beautiful home. The guests were seated in order of relevance and the food was artfully arranged. Everyone spoke English, as noted by Croatian artist Mladen Stilinovic in his 1992 work *An Artist Who Cannot Speak English Is No Artist*. A lot of art is about irony.

Until recently, inexpensive plane fares made it easy to move the body. With a lot of travel the psycho-cultural issues of displacement and isolation arrive later like network packets. For many young curators and artists, traveling the globe and living in new places is projected to be the most essential and meaningful of pursuits. Many mid-career Creatives are still attached to a romantic life of travel, harkening back to romantic literature and cinema. Travel has changed and the locations one romanticizes about have changed. The arts can have an unintentional consequence of opening up locations and then turning them inside out. Among the lions, tigers, elephants, and ungulates in the Serengeti is a Four Seasons Hotel. Culture is often confused with geography, and expats, especially those who are art related, create mini ghettos to construct the familiar and avoid the new. Familiarity is the most comforting of conditions and despite the apparent homogenization of the world on the surface, the sub-layers may not always mix well.

Travel and relocation are meaningful and important and this collection of essays doesn't say otherwise. It presents issues, liabilities, and considerations. It addresses various concerns of pursuit and belonging, and relocation as a form of avoidance. The collection discusses elective, emergency, and forced travel and the concerns of integration including speaking the local language as only the beginning of becoming part of a community.

With issues of looking different in a homogenous culture such as being Afro-American in Korea (one of our Outbound Residents) or if you blur your identity in a heterogeneous location such as New York City, you will likely be asked for directions or hear the local dialect of your language spoken on the street. If your travel allows you to avoid intimacy or involvement, the risk can be high. Sometimes it ends up being a search for one's self. Some cultures value privacy, while being alone is a sign of loneliness in others. Ignoring or denying differences, not understanding them, or imposing your own, can make life around you confusing, unpredictable, and less rich.

Our residency program at apexart is described as a "simulated move to another city." It sounds a bit theatrical, but the program is a cultural immersion done largely on one's own in a new city. In a bit of a reversal, our residents must be over 30 years old and have never been to the city they are sent. Additionally they are recommended by someone we approach, such as an adjunct faculty member in the city selected, in an effort to circumvent the "gate keeper" situation that the art world often creates in an exclusionary process. We do not provide a studio, no career networking, and no map with directions to Artistan's art locations. Rather than putting them in a restricted art environment studio doing the same thing they were doing before they arrived, we provide each resident with a rigorous schedule of social and cultural activities that they are expected to follow. We do set up meetings but they are not "promotional," and they are not intended to introduce the residents to Artistanians for a quid pro quo. These activities are generally outside their normal activities and interests and are intended to be catalytic experiences possibly to be incorporated into their work and/or life in some way. They might go to an "improv" acting class (self actualization and self challenging) or sit in on legal proceedings in a New York City courtroom (performance), after which a courtroom, judicial, or social reference may well appear in their work. During the month they are in residence they attend sessions with a licensed psychotherapist, which has not only proven to be one of the most popular activities, but one they may transfer in communication skills going forward.

The art world can often be very confining with an emphasis placed on "success" and this is an opportunity to address their personal concerns, in a foreign city—a sort of "stranger on a train" experience. Many of the activities they will do during one of our residencies in NYC are not available, culturally acceptable, or encouraged in their hometown or city. It is an empowering situation for people in many ways according to feedback from those who have participated. The idiosyncrasies and intentions of this program are too numerous to mention here and I refer you to our website for more information including sample daily schedules of Inbound Residents (to NYC), Outbound Residents (Africa, Brazil, Ethiopia, Australia, Cambodia, etc.), and personal journals provided by past residents.

We often travel in such a way that we seem to "hover" above the real world. We fly into Artistan International, go to the Artisanian restaurants that serve the art community with people we already know, and who were likely at the last fair or biennial. We tell others and ourselves how much we are doing while at the same time wondering what it is we are doing. In our modern culture you are either something or nothing and sometimes even both at the same time. It's pretty easy to be confused.

Some countries consistently dominate interest as others become transitional and certain countries attract artists. Berlin is the current hot city, New York and London had their time, and long ago there was Paris. The art world went through Italy, New York, Germany, then Russia. Recently smaller Eastern European cities such as Croatia and Ljubljana were centers of discussion. Not sure but right now it seems we are halfway through China. It's a moving marketplace and relocation always brings up personal issues of inclusion, rejection, and purpose. Skype helps, but it is not the same as real life integration. Often we cannot wait to get there and then cannot wait to leave. What does nationality mean in a place like Artistan? Is the currency hard or social? What is important and what is not? Travel and relocation encourages this kind of thinking. It's great that it does, though it's not always fun.

When we invite contributors to our publications, we ask that they be honest and personal about what they address, and to speak to you. apexart is not in service to our writers or the artists and curators with whom we work, we are in service to you, our audience. While you may be unique, many of your concerns are not, and just realizing that is good thing. We have similar feelings even as we have different issues. We often reality check by talking to others to see if they have the same response to something that you do. There are concerns you will read about herein that you have considered but may not have addressed. Your idea of success may change a bit or be reinforced.

Increasingly we live and value externally. We care too much about what others are thinking when in fact they are busy thinking of themselves and not us. We cannot be blamed for feeling that opportunity is based less on merit than personality—it happens. We are in a celebrity culture that does not distinguish between infamy and fame, at a time when society doesn't feel particularly friendly. I've followed an informal study of English youngsters' ambitions for almost 25 years. Five and six year olds answered the question of what they wanted to be when they grew up. Starting with policeman and fireman, it progressed with society to doctor and lawyer, then to businessman. In its most recent incarnation the kids switched from vocational to defensive. They answered "rich." Tough pursuit.

Our life is in a box. When we relocate we bring our virtual home with us. We bring our computer with our pictures, our music, our writing, our reading, and our news. Video chats have replaced the local TV station we once tried to watch in foreign countries to combat a sleep-shifted evening. We live a kind of travel trailer existence with our tech-based life. It allows us to not travel when we travel.

But the café has Wi-Fi and I'm happy.

Steven Rand (steven.rand@apexart.org) is an artist, writer, unlicensed architect, and general troublemaker living in NYC who tries to make the art world more creative and challenging through direct action and intervention.

Heather Felty

Introduction: Finding Home

With globalization theory on our minds for more than twenty years now and mobility becoming more commonplace, and even expected in contemporary art, it is no wonder our identities are bound up with our own sense of involvement in nomadism. We move so easily, and relatively freely, around the world that it has become normal to move to a new country for a job, to live somewhere temporarily, and to adapt readily, all while being required to understand cultural customs before we even get there. With all these expectations and exposure, how do we reconcile our own cultural identity? *Life Between Borders: The Nomadic Life of Curators and Artists* aims to consider the formation of identity in what has become the norm of a nomadic, migrating lifestyle.

Deleuze and Guattari have made a clear distinction between the nomad and the migrant, which is often cited in discussions on this topic. While migrating may be primarily for the destitute, we in the art field are certainly nomadic. We make our moves in pointed directions to every part of the world. Nearly everyone wants a piece of the nomadic action. The art world is a fairly privileged place, where people rarely migrate due to hardships. Traditionally nomads moved by ground in order to obtain food and livelihood. This has become the migrant life. Now, in the art field, we travel increasingly, not so much for our survival, but for exposure and making connections. We contemporary nomads moving around the field of art might follow the same cyclical pattern of movement as our ancestors, yet instead, we move through fairs, biennials, exhibitions, and the like. The more accustomed we become to travel, the easier it is to stay for longer periods. The more time we spend in one place, the greater exposure we gain to a different culture, language, and customs. And the more often we move, such exposure grows that much more. What happens to our identity when we progressively move from one place, one country, to the next, to live?

In thinking about how people are affected by living in foreign countries, among unknown cultures, I was curious to hear what others had experienced. As one who has enjoyed a fair share of moving, and a relative amount of culture shock along the way, I have asked myself many questions about the implications of moving on cultural identity, social acceptance, and the relatively recent intrigue in the art world of complex, multi-line bios. The authors of the following collected essays consider these questions and many more.

The idea of exploring the world and experiencing other cultures is romanticized on many levels. Nomads are celebrated in our society, and especially in the arts. Travel is seen as a sign of money, accomplishment, and opportunity. You have to be mobile to "make it" in the art world, which is constantly becoming smaller through this same travel. Artists are present at more international exhibitions than ever before, and artists' biographies include the birth location of the artist as well as where he or she is currently working/based. The itinerant lifestyle has become a new norm, yet both nomads and migrants have trouble fitting in, and must address issues of exclusion. Niels Van Tomme discusses this by way of examples of artists' works that critically reflect the migrant condition. On the other hand, it is easy for artists who travel the circuit to get caught up in the superficial aspects of moving from place to place, without identifying at all with the location. Gitanjali Dang suggests that artists not let constant moving distract themselves into believing that what is new is better. Pascal Gielen discusses the certain obligation artists have to travel, the romanticization of nomadic life, and reflects on how mobility increases chances for opportunities. Perhaps there is nothing wrong with artists using nomadism to their advantage. In relation to cultural diversity, it is important to understand how we connect with others, and to a new place. Lamia Joreige explains the ability to experience real encounters in an ever-moving age.

Despite a seeming correlation between travel and success, there is still an element of difficulty for some nomads. To outsiders it feels like you are there in the present, in the same reality, but you cannot really stop making references back to your previous experience, and locals can never fully understand your unique perspective. It doesn't matter if you moved across the ocean or to the next town over; there are always new neighbors, new stores, new references, new difficulties. It could be navigating your way through the grocery store, or keeping free from ethnic prejudices. As contemporary philosopher and feminist theoretician Rosi Braidotti has suggested, "we have to stop looking at immigration as a problem and see it as simply a fact of globalization." But tell that to the extremists. Nomads and migrants who travel for work face additional obstacles when the country they have moved to has even a small portion of the population that wants to maintain a "pure" ethnic race in our ever-migrating world.

The authors of the essays in this book reveal elements of their unique nomadic journeys. Yannis Ziogas shares his experience of his annual hiking project, highlighting some of the risks people face when moving by foot. Danger allows people to see their limitations and either try to move beyond them, or accept them. Ziogas describes piles of clothing discarded by migrants as they prepare for their new life. Children of migrants and nomads have a deeper notion of the implications of moving. Sebastien Sanz de Santamaria discusses his personal story of growing up as a global nomad, showcasing the moment, as a young teenager, when he was informed that he was bound to never be able to settle down. How do people identify themselves culturally after constantly moving as children? Mahita El Bacha Urieta, also sharing her personal story of growing up a global nomad, says that the "most reliable home might be within ourselves." For those who move a lot, they have to consider what happens to their "treasured" possessions during their moves, and determine what sacrifices to make in terms of attachment and adaptation. Jimmie Durham shares his method of keeping a library as a nomad as a means to maintain one's identity.

While there is widespread debate on the benefits of borders being removed—for either migration or economic reasons—it seems quite unlikely that English will ever become the only language the world speaks, even if it is our common language. On the question of culture and language on identity, in light of increasing global migration, to what degree will nationality inform identity? Will we always try to hold on to who we are based on where we are from, or will that view be relaxed? If we are tied to our "home," then we are faced with a perpetual desire to be in one's home country, which some of the authors here have addressed. Some languages have one word to describe this feeling: Mahita El Bacha Urieta discusses the French word *dépaysement*; in Greek, the word is *nostos*; in Portugese, *saudade*; other languages have their equivalents; curiously there is no one-word English translation. I've often wondered what role language plays in identity and fitting in, as it is natural to not be fully connected without knowing the local language. Mekbib Gemeda shares his experience of moving to different countries and how language influences adaptability to culture. If you do not keep up a language, do you lose some connection to that culture?

Globalization has led us to eclectic bios being ordinary while inter-cultural marriages, bi-national children, and visa-free travel blur the lines of how we speak of "we" in relation to where someone is from, and how long someone has been in a certain place (relative to remaining an outsider).

Melissa Chiu evaluates how cultural differences can be seen in various countries through the examination of exhibitions that showcase the art world's interest in the Other, addressing the issue of how much time the curator spends in a place to recognize the culture. Chiu suggests there is a curatorial imperative to understand the cultural context.

We can determine our identity through our nationality, our heritage, what languages we know, how long we have maintained residence in different countries, among many other influences. Once someone has found his or her comfort zone in relation to these aspects, through navigating language and customs, as well as infrastructure, there will be a certain level of struggle or culture shock and certain expectations until either a comfort zone is found, or we return "home." No matter how often we move, or where we move to, it is not the place that changes; the change occurs within us. Identity is our choice to define as we see fit; nomadism provides an opportunity for us to be exposed to other cultures and people, which contributes to our cultural identity.

With most of us having moved to either another city, or another country, and having learned a language or two beyond our mother tongue, the essays in this book will resonate with nearly every reader. We hope that you find inspiration in these ideas and will use the book as a resource to spark further investigation into this ever-evolving topic.

Heather (Kouris) Felty has been affiliated with apexart since 1999 in various core capacities. She writes and has curated several exhibitions and has been living between borders for half her life.

Pascal Gielen

Nomadeology: The Aestheticization of Nomadic Existence

On the one hand the cosmopolitan upper- and upper-middle-class academic, always with the proper visas enabling him to cross borders without any problem in order to carry out his (financial, academic...) business, and thus able to "enjoy the difference"; on the other hand the poor (im)migrant worker driven from his home by poverty or (ethnic, religious) violence, for whom the celebrated "hybridity" designates a very tangible traumatic experience of never being able to settle down properly and legalize his status, the subject for who such simple tasks as crossing a border or reuniting with his family can be an experience full of anxiety...[1]

Black Planet

A few years ago, the Amsterdam designer Thomas Buxò proposed a remarkable version of the map of the world to me. The bright blue color of the water and the white, reddish-brown, and green that usually represent the landmasses on such maps were replaced by a uniform, pitch-black background. Shining like little stars in this dark area, which no longer showed any distinction between land and water, were white dots that marked the international art biennials of the past decade. In addition to this strange typology, dots also indicated the locations of closed asylum centers. The fact that Western Europe was especially bright in Buxò's world might not be surprising, but besides another noticeable concentration of dots in Japan, what particularly struck the eye was the darkness in Africa.

This world looked *unheimlich*, and not just because it emphasized for the umpteenth time that the distribution of wealth easily corresponds with that of art and art tourism. What especially evoked an uncomfortable feeling was the geographical proximity of art biennials and asylum centers. It underscored the fact that the right to travel, and more in general to mobility, is not inalienable for everybody on this globe. Moreover, the geopolitical areas where this right is both granted and denied are not all that equally distributed across the world. The junctions where travel bans are imposed and where travel is encouraged as an ideal way of life lie abhorrently close to one another. Obligatory but unwanted nomads on the one hand, voluntary and socially encouraged nomads on the other, can almost see, smell, and touch one another. The last, however, is usually strictly forbidden by law, or at least made physically difficult or even completely impossible. The careful political segregation of globetrotters has a bitter taste. Against this background, the excessive enthusiasm for nomadism that has occupied the discourse in the art world for the past 15 years begins to seem rather unreal.

Nomads & Nomads

"This is all fantastic for artists—they are no longer duty-bound by family commitments to work locally… and the open market allows them to travel fairly freely, give or take a visa or two. You could say we are becoming highly networked."[2]

'Rizhomatic,' 'global drift,' 'dislocated,' 'diaspora,' 'unbelonging,' 'connectivity,' 'networks,' 'deterritorialization,' 'exodus,' 'cosmopolitanism,' and of course 'nomad' are part of a discursive universe with which artists and independent curators have been describing their practices for some time now. Just browse through a few catalogues of international exhibitions and you will soon come across the romanticism of the homeless person. With or without giving it a Deleuzo-Guattarian gloss, the protagonists in one part of Buxò's black world like to describe and promote their activities and events in a sophisticated 'nomadeology.' For the record, this term must not be confused with 'nomadology' without an 'e,' the title of the similarly-named chapter from the classic *A Thousand Plateaus* by Gilles Deleuze and Félix Guattari.[3] What particularly concerns me is the extremely one-sided interpretation of this nomadology. In the art world and elsewhere, this interpretation is literally one-sided, seeing as Deleuze and Guattari indicate at least two 'camps,' or in their terms, two possible 'war machines' in nomadology. Both fight against the State but from entirely different positions—more on that later, though. The point is that the positive aura that today is fairly smoothly generated around travel, mobility, agility, unattachment, and even homelessness makes it likely that the term has become part of an ideology, which is why I speak of 'nomadeology.'

In any case, artists and curators nowadays are morally obliged to leave their familiar biotope and seek an uncertain but always inspiring Elsewhere. To accommodate them, artist-in-residencies form interconnecting points all over the world, and the earlier-mentioned biennials along with international art centers and museums provide the trusted scenes in which these creative world travellers can regularly meet up with one another.[4] Cheap plane tickets take away every excuse; artists must explore the wild blue yonder. The period when travelling around the world was exclusively reserved for an elitist jet set or for the time-honored cosmopolitan with a considerable inheritance in his or her pocket is a page of history that was turned some time ago. How long this new period will last, nobody knows. For the moment, the continuing financial crisis has not yet caused the price of plane tickets to rise too drastically, and the looming ecological crash has not yet instilled enough fear in us to make us stay on the ground *en masse*.

But this is certainly not just about physical travel. Artists have always had a fascination for nomads. We already find this in some descriptions of 19th century artist-bohemians and flâneurs, but recent artists and photographers have also liked to portray vagabonds and other homeless people. Thus, nomadism is both an example for artists' lives and a subject for their art.

This can include both a romantic view of gypsy life, such as in the work of British photographer Iain McKell, or a solicitude for the continued existence of nomadic peoples, such as in the documentary work of Dutchman Jeroen Toirkens. Or what to think of British artist Lucy Orta, who developed 'refugee fashion,' a kind of survival kit for the modern nomad including nylon coffins and 'ready-to-wear outfits for an atomic winter'?

What is striking, as I have said, is the contemporary art world's one-sided appropriation of the nomadic discourse. Why are so many positive characteristics ascribed to nomadic life? And why does this so easily lead to self-identification—at least verbally—in the case of most artists and independent curators? After all, media reports on the fate of the Roma, fugitives, and 'bona fide refugees' hardly present a pretty picture. If they haven't already become victims of racist football supporters or the violence of ordinary local citizens, governments will dump perpetual travellers and fugitives in camps and ghettos in order to discourage integration (as in Italy) or enter them in secret ethnic registers strongly reminiscent of the eve of World War II (as in the Netherlands). In a world in which alien offices assume that an asylum seeker is by definition a liar until he or she proves otherwise, and in which refugees are preferably deported or thrown overboard, the nomadic life does not really offer much to be jealous about. "History has always dismissed the nomads," assert Deleuze and Guattari.[5]

Against the background of this philosophical science in combination with the empirical facts, the 'lifestyle-nomadism' and 'exile-romanticism' of many contemporary artists and curators sound somewhat obscene. This glorification of the nomadic life comes across as misplaced in an era when desperate people are relocated from one condemned building to the next socio-economically depressed area.[6] It is easy for artists or curators who are the products of the middle or upper classes to extol a homeless existence when they have a credit card and the proper visas in their pockets.

At least it should be clear that nowadays there are different sorts of nomads. An important distinction can be made between two groups: those who are forced to move and those who do so voluntarily. The latter group tends to leave the *Heimat* from a comfortable position, both financially and socially. Whether this second group, to which the earlier-mentioned curators and artists mostly belong, can so easily identify with the first sort of nomad is a very big question. A purely discursive and romantic identification with real stateless and homeless people leads to an aestheticization of the nomadic existence. In the same way that Walter Benjamin[7] pointed out the problem of the aestheticization of politics in fascism, here we can pose the question of whether the aestheticization of the nomadic existence does not in fact serve the prevailing neoliberal hegemony, including post-Fordist working conditions.

Mobile Loner

Both Richard Sennett[8] and Luc Boltanski & Eve Chiapello[9] argue that the economic policy which is currently spreading across the globe actually welcomes the mobile person with open arms. Especially when that mobile man or woman is employable for the further accumulation of capital. Boltanski and Chiapello even claim that nowadays mobility is one of the most important discriminating factors around which a new kind of class segregation is taking shape. The more mobile people and their products are, the more chance they have of getting ahead. On the other hand, people who for one reason or another are tied to a locality have fewer possibilities of working themselves higher up the ladder. This is why the social mobility of women is still lower than that of men, because statistically speaking they are still more tied to their children and family than their partners are. And this is also why speculators and investors can grow rich more easily than business owners and corporate directors, who are tied to their means of production.

Money is simply much more mobile than machines, conveyor belts, personnel, and other means of production. Those who are only involved with speculation can reposition their efforts much more easily and quickly than those who have to deal with relocating an entire factory. Flows of capital, which thanks to today's digital transactions race around the globe at lightning speed, have made the world liquid. They obligate both employers and workers to quickly and flexibly take advantage of new market demands, and therefore new work situations. This is why economic fugitives are not the only ones who chase after capital. Entrepreneurs and corporate directors are also being increasingly forced to relocate their production centers, while managers feel obligated to change their employer and workplace once every five to seven years—that is, if they want to continue moving up the social ladder.

A nomadic existence is extremely functional for an economy driven less by production, or even consumption, and increasingly by a hyper-dynamic of liquid assets. And as we know, individuals are more mobile than collectives, such as entire production units, teams, but also families. What is more, the 'lone' nomad cannot fall back on unions and other collective assurances of solidarity that are so bothersome for employers. In short, the current neoliberal hegemony that keeps the global casino going with extremely virtual games has every interest in declaring its players outlaws. The individual nomad fits that profile perfectly. Then why would the art world want to go along with this nomadeology by gathering a positive morality around this highly vulnerable mobile person?

Idealism and Individualism

Free movement of thought necessarily implies not always clinging to what is known and perceived as functional and "right," what has been practiced or experienced previously. Working from the outside, like a non-institutionalized free agent—who is, to a certain extent, comparable to an external consultant—also means actively performing a certain marginality. The isolation of such marginality can only be overcome by a relentless will for collaboration, a commitment and willingness to change things—beyond intellectual aspirations, but through significant distance that produces a mode of criticality, a distance that an insider cannot offer and does not possess.[10]

The nomad, the traveller or the 'uninvited outsider,' as architect Markus Miessen calls such individuals, have certain qualities that can call the above-mentioned hegemony into question. Of all people, the outsider has the possibility of taking a commanding view of outmoded local patterns and introducing possible changes. No one can position themselves above their own society. Outsiders such as nomads, however, have the advantage of an alternative way of looking at things, simply because their cultural background is different. Not only Miessen, but also artists like Francis Alÿs[11] understand only too well that it is precisely the 'in between' position of nomads that makes it possible for them to visualize what others do not see. Moreover, they can more easily mediate in conflict situations where those involved are too biased to take a 'neutral' position. In other words, the previously posited nomadeology, or the neoliberal hegemony's embrace of the mobile person, does not prevent the nomad model from being deployed in a counter-hegemony. Deleuze and Guattari also make a distinction between two types of nomads, who in their story stand outside the State:

> The outside appears simultaneously in two directions: huge worldwide machines branched out over the entire ecumenon at a given moment, which enjoy a large measure of autonomy in relation to the States (for example, commercial organizations of the 'multinational' type, or industrial complexes, or even religious formations like Christianity, Islam, certain prophetic or messianic movements, etc.) but also the local mechanisms of bands, margins, minorities, which continue to affirm the rights of segmentary societies in opposition to the organs of State power.[12]

It seems only natural that the art world would identify with the second type of nomad. In any case, we find such an idealistic identification in Miessen's Winter School Middle East project and in Alÿs's walks and poetic activities. Both use nomadic strategies specifically in order to escape the prevailing hegemony or break regional stalemates. Here, nomadism is courting a form of interventionism that we know from the history of the Situationists, but then on a worldwide scale. And just like the Situationists, these artistic nomads take the risk of becoming completely caught up in the political 'war machine.' When they take this risk with conviction, however, there must be no doubting their sincere idealism.

The question remains, though, whether such a strategy and nomadic position are actually very effective politically. The designations that Miessen,[13] for instance, uses to indicate his protagonists, such as 'freelancer with a consciousness,' 'crossbench politician,' 'non-institutionalized free-agent,' or 'external consultant,' can be considered highly ambivalent to say the least. The freelancer and the consultant do not just meet with pampering in today's post-Fordist and neoliberal regime. What's more, their responsibility is only temporary, and their position dependent on the good will of varying employers. Whether their so-called autonomy, which in fact is an extremely dependent and precarious professional position, allows them to take any political risks is very much the question. Just as the original 'freelancer' was a person who was hired to fight with a lance, nowadays consultants and free agents are only hirelings in the present neoliberal hegemony. And as we know, hirelings historically have had very little idealism or conscience. These qualities are quite simply dysfunctional when it comes to their survival. But even if there were freelancers with a conscience or consultants with an ideal, as Miessen believes there are, it is still doubtful whether such positions offer them the necessary strength and power to actually generate political effects. Their highly individual position, which is not institutionally embedded and which therefore can hardly count on collective support, is precisely what makes this type of nomad particularly weak in every social and political struggle. If the Roma, the Jews in exodus, gypsies, and other ambulatory hordes have been able to accumulate a modicum of political power in their long nomadic history, it was only because they were part of a relatively sizable collective. Or, as Deleuze and Guattari expressly state in their fifth proposition: "Nomad existence necessarily implies the numerical elements of a war machine."[14] Their great numbers and common exodus are precisely why the Roma and other gypsies have not always remained so invisible and ignored. It is doubtful whether the individual nomadism of consultants, freelancers, or free agents could develop sufficient strength to accumulate any appreciable political influence. As individuals, they are too weak for that, and moreover, too dependent on the economic caprices of an environment with constantly varying principals.

And this brings us back to artists. Since the modern age, they too have claimed a highly individual position. At the end of the 19th century, this inflated to the proportion of the romantic bohemian artist. According to rather biographical myths, such an eccentric regularly navigated a vagabond middle course between insider and outsider, between maniac and genius, between drunkard and whoremonger on the one hand and prominent, even authoritative citizen on the other. One reason why artists earned that last, positive status was because despite all their idiosyncrasies they also managed to incorporate the prevailing values of a liberal civil society. After all, individual freedom and authenticity were of paramount importance to liberalism, which not coincidentally gained its definitive outlines in the 19th century together with the modern artist. Art and market capitalism have had a good relationship with each other from the moment that people were willing to pay money for artistic artifacts. But in their classic study, *Canvases and Careers*,[15] sociologists Cynthia and Harrison White convincingly show that the market did not really begin to play a central role until after the decline of the academic model.

According to the authors, when the system of the Parisian Académie royale de Peinture et Sculpture and the annual salon burst apart under morphological pressure, this enabled the birth of what they call the 'dealer-critic' system. Not only did art criticism now gain an important role; the status of the artist also radically changed under the influence of the market. The artist's personal style became more important than submission to a uniform system of rules. What was relevant now was not a single, annually-submitted prospective masterpiece, but a coherent oeuvre that guaranteed the lasting quality of the artist. To put it in a slightly different way, when the Académie lost its monopoly, the bets were no longer placed on masterpieces; instead, the individual careers of the artists themselves came to the foreground. Or, as the title of White and White's study clearly underscores, the central focus in the post-academic system was not the artists' canvases but their careers. Behind these shifts, however, lies a simple capitalistic market logic. After all, the potential buyer must be convinced of the quality of an art work. At that point, the most important arguments a seller can use to convince the buyer are the above-mentioned critique of the work on the one hand and the perception of the success of earlier works on the other. In other words, quality which has been previously produced in an oeuvre functions as a promise of future quality.

What is important here is that our contemporary concepts of 'the individual artist' and 'authorship' are partly a product of the marketing of the art world. The artist as authentic individual is historically supported by a liberal bourgeois ideal, the artist as nomad by a similarly bourgeois cosmopolitanism. In the contemporary art world, that model easily transforms into a parochial (because middle-class) ideal of *Rough Guide* backpack consumer exoticism. As such, the would-be artist can sharpen his or her creativity by travelling relatively easily to the Other. In other words, a liberal-bourgeois ideal simply transmutes to a neoliberal consumption-individualism in this day and age.

If artists really want to escape this political-ideological framework, like Alÿs and Miessen, then it seems necessary to go a step further. Not only must they relinquish their own cultural and national identity, as in nomadism, but also the claim to individualism made by almost every artistic practice until now. Individualism was a mistake. For a truly politically effective nomadism, individualism must be sacrificed to the collectivity of Deleuze and Guattari's 'war machine.' Or in their histrionics: "You have to be born a slave, to become a soldier."[16] This is not to say, however, that artistry should be given up, but that authorship must be set free. An artistic act can only be politically effective when it is a singular act. That is, when an act is set free of an individual owner and thus becomes truly autonomous. Such a singular autonomous act is immediately available to the commons. From there, it can assemble with other singular energies in order to be collectively appropriated and politically deployed.

In any case, an artistic work that is in the possession of the artist, a collector, or a museum remains politically impotent when it cannot be appropriated by others. This also holds true for art works that ostensibly intervene in public space, that explicitly propagate a political message, and even works that lead a risky existence in war zones. When artists do not generously make their works available to the people they visit or identify with, when they instead claim individuality and authorship, they immediately make themselves available to the first group of nomads that Deleuze and Guattari speak of: commercial businesses, the creative industry, and the multinational art market. Certainly now that the State—unlike how the French philosophers conceived of it over 20 years ago—is increasingly putting itself at the service of this capitalistic 'war machine,' it is necessary to institute a much more strongly articulated multitude. Today it is not so much the State that is confronting the nomadic war machine, as was the case with Deleuze and Guattari, but 'war machine' confronting 'war machine.' After all, the neoliberal State has chosen to dissolve itself by choosing the camp of the multinationals. As a result, the two kinds of nomads are confronting one another in an increasingly clear manner.

Considering this irreversible reality of capitalism's appropriation of the ambulatory person and the State, one has to conclude that nomadism as an artistic strategy only makes political sense if it is communist. For the record, this loaded word does not refer to the historical state communism, as we knew it in the U.S.S.R., nor to the authoritarian one-party policy that we still see in China today. On the contrary, the communism referred to here is stateless, precisely because it is nomadic. This is the communistic ideal (Deleuze and Guattari would have spoken of a 'thought,' which according to them is always nomadic), that has been elaborated by the French philosopher Alain Badiou,[17] among others. Communism then amounts to a universal call to radical equality in an endless variety of forms.

Only when artists' journeys reveal inequalities, and when their singular artistic acts make them part of collective emancipatory subjectivities, does this nomadism come alive politically. However, these artists cannot hide behind a neutral artistic position but will have to choose sides. So they must no longer noncommittally 'make things visible' without showing their colors, without passing judgment (how often haven't I heard artists say that their work has 'no judgmental intention'). In any event, artists certainly cannot lay any historical weight on the scales if they do not bury their ego politics of individualism.

Of course, artists do not have to be political. Of course, they can use trips to exotic places, instructive dialogues, and residencies with a wealth of experience in the Other to simply stimulate their creativity, expand their networks, and make careers for themselves. Of course, they can refuse nomadic communism and use their love of travel to soak up the Other and make it their own, in order to build up a strong individuality and artistic identity. There is nothing wrong with this. However, when they identify with the fortunes of the stateless, the sufferings of the Roma, and the misery of refugees, or when they move through conflict zones without passing political judgment, it becomes dubious. Then their empathy and 'engagement' only serve as a way of getting their own artistic advantage out of it, and thus enriching themselves. When artists are tempted to do this, their activities go no further than age-old colonial practices. However ambulatory, engaged, or politically radical their work may appear to be, ultimately it remains caught up in the neoliberal war machine. Then the nomadic adventure serves nothing but personal self-enrichment, and the nomadic rhetoric is no more than a handy marketing strategy.

NOTES

1. Slavoj Žižek, *Ticklish Subject. The Absent Centre of Political Ontology* (London and New York: Verso, 2000), 220.
2. Carolyn Black, *Cultural Identity and the Nomadic Artist* http://www.a-n.co.uk:81/nan/article/209957/209954 (2005), 1.
3. Gilles Deleuze and Félix Guattari, *A Thousand Plateaus. Capitalism and Schizophrenia* (London: The Athlone Press, 1988).
4. Pascal Gielen, *The Murmuring of the Artistic Multitude. Global Art, Memory and Post-Fordism* (Amsterdam: Valiz, 2009).
5. Gilles Deleuze and Félix Guattari, *Nomadology: The War Machine* (Seattle: Warmwood Distribution, 2010), 63.
6. Bavo, *Too Active to Act. Cultureel activisme na het einde van de geschiedenis* (Amsterdam: Valiz, 2010): 59.
7. William Benjamin, *Selected Writings. Volume 4 – 1938-1940* (Cambridge, MA and London: The Belknap Press of Harvard University Press, 2003).
8. Richard Sennett, *The Corrosion of Character. The Personal Consequences of Work in the New Capitalism* (New York: Norton, 1998).
9. Luc Boltanski & Eve Chiapello, *The New Spirit of Capitalism* (London and New York: Verso, 2005).
10. Markus Miessen, *The Nightmare of Participation (Crossbench Praxis as a Mode of Criticality)* (Berlin: Sternberg Press, 2010), 240-242.
11. See T.J. Demos, "Vanishing Mediator," in *Francis Alÿs. A Story of Deception* ed. Mark Godfrey (London: Tate, 2010), pp. 178-180, for example.
12. Gilles Deleuze and Félix Guattari, *Nomadology: The War Machine* (Seattle: Warmwood Distribution, 2010), 15.

13. Markus Miessen, *The Nightmare of Participation (Crossbench Praxis as a Mode of Criticality)* (Berlin: Sternberg Press, 2010), 240-242.

14. Gilles Deleuze and Félix Guattari, *Nomadology: The War Machine* (Seattle: Warmwood Distribution, 2010), 54.

15. Harrison C. White and Cynthia A. White, *Canvases and Careers. Institutional Change in the French Painting World* (Chicago and London: The University of Chicago Press, 1965).

16. Gilles Deleuze and Félix Guattari, *Nomadology: The War Machine* (Seattle: Warmwood Distribution, 2010), 62.

17. Alain Badiou, *L'Hypothèse Communiste* (Paris: Nouvelles Editions Lignes, 2009).

Pascal Gielen (1970) is director of the research center Arts in Society at the Groningen University where he is Associate Professor Sociology of Art. Gielen also leads the research group and book series *Arts in Society* (Fontys School of Fine and Performing Arts, Tilburg). He has written several books on contemporary art, cultural heritage, and cultural politics. In 2009 Gielen edited together with Paul De Bruyne the book *Being an Artist in Post-Fordist Times* (NAi) and he published the monograph *The Murmuring of the Artistic Multitude: Global Art, Memory and Post-Fordism* (Valiz). In 2011 De Bruyne and Gielen edited the book *Community Art: The Politics of Trespassing* and in January 2012 their book *Teaching Art in the Neoliberal Realm: Realism versus Cynicism* was launched. In 2013 Gielen's new monograph *Creativity and other Fundamentalisms*, and the reader *Institutional Attitudes: Instituting Art in a Flat World* (ed. Gielen) will come out. Gielen's research focuses on cultural politics and the institutional contexts of the arts.

Lamia Joreige

Real Encounters

It is often said today that artists of every stripe are more nomadic than ever. One can react to this reality in a number of ways. On the one hand, it could be said that nomadism has caused a homogenization of the global community; for example, even though one may travel all the way from New York to Beijing, it is still common to encounter people who are very similar to each other—despite their cultural diversity. On the other hand, one might emphasize the diversification of identities encouraged by nomadism; for example, since artists are constantly engaged in encountering other artists, they are thus pushed to reflect on their own practices and on their identities in order to recreate them constantly. I think much is correct about these two positions; indeed, many interesting things could be and, in fact, are said about nomadism from them. Nevertheless, I do not want to analyze the causes and the effects of such nomadism from a sociological, economical, or anthropological point of view. Instead, despite the relevance of these approaches, I want to address the matter from my very subjective perspective as an artist: I want to question the value that such nomadism (or what is commonly called nomadism) has in relation to the specific question of what I call a *real encounter*; in what ways does itinerancy shape the kinds of encounters artists have today? Is what lies beneath a nomadic lifestyle the hope for an encounter?

In *A Thousand Plateaus*, Deleuze and Guattari oppose the nomad to the figure of the migrant: whereas the former is understood to be rootless, in a state of vital displacement and is only properly understood in terms of trajectories, the migrant becomes a sort of tourist, a visitor of locations with often only the practical on his or her mind. I am tempted to say that the circuitous nomadism of today's artists resembles the migrant more than the nomad on Deleuze and Guattari's terms. The migrant, like any traveler, is easily categorized; he poses no problem of recognition upon arrival or departure. As for the nomad, however, there seems to be a breakdown in such mechanisms of recognition: he fails to demonstrate the correct knowledge at certain circumstances and, in fact, appears to be totally ignorant of customs and obligations. How can such a figure become a transmitter of another culture? This touches on the possible uses of language in such circumstances; what if an artist is ignorant of linguistic conventions or norms that dictate expression? What if an artist employs terms and concepts idiosyncratically and thus distorts the preconceptions of others? I believe that something like this contributes toward a *real encounter*, and that it may exist, although not exclusively, in a kind of figure of artist that does not travel. I don't mean to idealize this figure in any way—or suggest that artists should follow that example, but I want to emphasize that *there was something originally valuable about nomadism which seems to have been diminished in being transposed to another concept like migration: we lose the possibility of real encounter*.

In 2009, I was invited to be a resident at the Serpentine Gallery in London as part of the Edgware Road project, and I was encouraged to produce a work that engaged with the history of that neighborhood and its diversity. Though I accepted this invitation and was eager to participate, it so happened that I could not produce anything; eventually, I realized that this had to do with my being outside Beirut, and it became clear to me that my methods and practices, which had grown and developed in Beirut, were, for this very reason, ineffectual in London. Consequently, I experienced a strong tension between my incapacity to engage with the new city and my desire to displace my practices and methods; what was keeping me from fulfilling this displacement was that I did not have a deep enough experience with and knowledge of London—or rather, I lacked the type of irrational attachment that I have to Beirut as well as the desire to portray and reflect on my home town. In a word, I was simply not "seduced" by the city, and I neither had the desire to produce anything about it nor in it. Although I proceeded to make use of some of the methods common in my work, methods which I use in my own city such as collecting filmed notes and archival documents, and filming hours-long sequence shots in order to capture the passage of life and time in a specific location, I remained alienated from the work I was invited to create. In the end, this problem led me to consider including my very inability to engage with London as a part of the work I would eventually produce.

I am recounting this story because I want to know if that situation even offered a real ground for the type of interaction I was hoping to have in the first place, or if, *de facto*, it was an illusory opportunity. Given the way things happened, I began asking, on what common grounds artists can effectively communicate their cultivated practices without reducing the value of their contribution.

In my case, the residency lasted a few months, and yet I was still unable to make the impact I would have hoped for; this makes me wonder about even shorter opportunities such as festivals and biennials—are encounters possible within that context? Although artists are not asked to create works at these kinds of situations, there arises another (related) question: How is encountering others artists and their work possible in such circumstances that are even more intensely compact; where people are rushing around seeing so many works in just a couple of hours, greeting acquaintances, meeting colleagues and friends?

These reflections push me to ask a question. Given that we so desire to encounter the other in our nomadic life/work-styles, what are the conditions for an encounter to genuinely occur? And what do I mean by encounter? It seems that this word has different meanings, and I wonder if it is possible that what many people today consider to be an encounter between artists or between practices is perhaps an illusory encounter? I see three aspects to this illusion that are worth discussing.

The sacredness of the Artist's presence

When it is possible, the presence of an artist during the showing of their work is almost universally preferred—almost required; this has to do with reasons that range from logistical concerns of setting up the work for exhibition, to the common belief in the aura generated by the artist's presence, a presence which can often be overdone. Often times, artists, curators, and spectators alike make the assumption that the artist's presence somehow ensures a fuller expression of the piece being exhibited just by being there physically— that his or her physical presence contributes to the meaning of the work exhibited; in fact, it is usually the case that the artist is often coping with practical matters, and engaging in a number of publicity-related activities such as advertising the work or advocating it in some generic manner. In short, physical presence does not imply the kind of mental presence required to fully express the meaning of a work; but people seem to forget this, and when they do they make a curious logical leap from the physical presence of the artist to the supposed full expression of the work exhibited.

In the case of the residency, perhaps something similar could be said since it was taken for granted that the presence of different invited artists working on site would contribute to a new reading of Edgware Road's history;

when perhaps there is an inherent difficulty with taking artists out of their habitual contexts and asking them to work as artists in other places.

The possibility of sharing

Another thing that gets emphasized about nomadic lifestyles in the arts is the way different perspectives can be shared more easily than ever before. Indeed, rather than having secluded communities of artists discussing matters in very particularized ways, we see today the growth of an exchange of ideas between what could have been isolated groups of artists. However, I think that, just as with the presence of the artist, this advantage can also be illusory. Consider the way that during large artistic events like festivals and biennials, it is common that everyone speaks a language in which artistic references can be universally understood. This language eventually comes to have a life of its own; so much so that when one is in such a general setting it is important to ask how much of their specificity can be properly shared? This can happen at both the level of the artist's identity, and also on the level of the meaning of a single work; these two get taken up in the general context of an event and often fail to transmit what provided the meaning of the work for them in the first place. I am not saying that this is all that happens; rather, I am stressing that there is a dangerous way in which this can—and indeed, does—occur. I therefore ask, is there a *false faith* that the specificity of cultures and of works can be transmitted adequately through a homogenized international language? I could list many examples such as when I was invited to participate in an artistic event and I ended up becoming a kind of cultural transmitter from which the audience was to learn about Lebanon, and my country's politics, customs, etc.—in some ways, even my work was reduced to that. No doubt, my work is grounded in Lebanon and its socio-political context, but that does not warrant such a narrow interpretation. It is easy to get caught in a situation where one's background causes one to become totally defined by certain cultural, political, historical contexts, i.e., wars, revolutions, etc., that are taking place in one's country. What results from this kind of misapprehension is an illusory feeling that one has encountered the other, when in fact they have instead succeeded in summarizing this other in familiar terms; and any radical difference that may stand out gets dismissed or dulled.

The Myth of an International Community

Taken together, the presence of the artist and the efficiency of a homogenized international language gives rise to the obvious conclusion that a community has been birthed; a community, in this sense, is a group in which all interests and beliefs are adequately reflected so that particular differences are recognized by others. Today, we speak of a Global Community as if it was a fact, but it is beginning to dawn on many that perhaps this is just a slogan that covers over essential inequalities and misunderstandings. Admittedly, the art community is far more open to diversity than most other organizations; in this respect, it actually seems that the art community, if it exists, succeeds in acting as a community insofar as particular differences are not ignored and are in fact celebrated. There is therefore belief in an ideal circumstance in which artists, while maintaining what is specific to their identities, can come together and share something in common. This is definitely a positive thing, but do we not risk a dilution of the specificity of the artists and their work in all this mutual recognition in the other? If one is taken up by the enthusiasm of sharing a common 'language' or an artistic practice with someone else, for instance, are they not tempted to shed those aspects of their work and personal life that are not homogeneous with this international context?

The main thing that I wish to emphasize about the nomadism of artists today is that it is related to both the sacredness of the presence of the artists as well as on the assumption of cultural sharing such that the idea of community contributes to an illusory encounter. I think that we are often led to believe that if these three factors attain, then we are to experience a real encounter amongst artists and between works, when in fact this rarely occurs.

So how does a *real encounter occur*? From my experience, it can take place when a displacement of methods and practices is experienced by those who take part in the encounter—when something feels awkward, but is nevertheless pursued by both (or all) parties. Displacement of a practice—as I have come to see it—involves making use of some artistic method without anticipating its reception; in so far as artists are pushed to consider the impact of their work on an audience and seek out ways to homogenize their forms of expression with those of the others, then I believe they could in fact minimize the chances of a real encounter taking place. What I mean is that a *real encounter* involves the employment of the methods familiar to an artist without anticipating the way that they will be understood, i.e., without tweaking them to plan and facilitate the reception of one's work by a foreign audience.

Although language remains one of the central means by which artists can come to express the meaning of their works, an important feature of Displacement is when participants in an encounter accept the impossibility of a common language that is adequate to both and see that this is as a crucial part of the encounter in question—not an obstacle for it. Making the work itself becomes the ground for that encounter.

Finally, it is important not to confuse the possibility of making a real encounter with the time spent in a particular location; in a manner reminiscent of love, *encounters* can occur in a moment's breath, leaving much that is either ungraspable or irreducible beyond that moment. Throughout all my reflections, I have not wanted to explain how this is possible (for how does one describe something at once so specific and intangible?), so much as I wanted to question the absolute value of a nomadic lifestyle and its possibility of providing for such an encounter between artists and the works that they travel with. I believe that there is no direct relationship between today's itinerant lifestyles and the sort of encounter artists deeply value between each other; such engagement is the product of something else.

Deleuze and Guattari importantly emphasize that the nomad does not move, if motion is understood in terms of migration from one point to another or across a circuit. In this way, taken metaphorically, the artist who does not travel can be a lesson for other artists. There might be something to be admired about this artist who stays put, who refuses to learn and speak an international language, who refuses to be reduced to one's identity. Would not such an approach perhaps enhance the capacity of an encounter?

The author wishes to thank Muhannad Hariri for his contribution to this text.

Lamia Joreige is a visual artist and filmmaker who lives and works in Beirut. She uses archival documents and fictitious elements to reflect on the relation between individual stories and collective History. She explores the possibilities of representation of the Lebanese wars and their aftermath, and Beirut, a city at the center of her imagery. Her work is essentially on Time, the recordings of its trace and its effects on us. She is a co-founder and co-director of Beirut Art Center, a unique non-profit space dedicated to contemporary art in Lebanon.

Jimmie Durham

Building a Nomadic Library

Last month I was reading Italo Calvino's *Six Lectures for the New Millennium* (wherein he asks, "Why do people always say they are 're-reading' the classics?"). He writes about building a library of classics, and it got me to thinking about my reading habits in general.

I have been a constant reader for many years, having picked up the habit in the military when Eisenhower was president of the U.S. You might wonder how I survived; the books available were a strange mix: Mickey Spillane, Ian Fleming, Ayn Rand, Eric Hoffer, I think, but also an anthology of poetry edited by Oscar Williams. I discovered English poetry.

Since the 1950s I have never lived very long in any one place and have never had very much money. With little formal education I've not known how to find books. They are always paperback and always what has been available in popular bookstores, train stations, and airports.

There have been exceptions. In the 60s an old woman gave me a set of *Encyclopedia Britannica* from the year 1900. It was in bad condition, but still a beautiful set. I read it every evening after work for many months. There were illustrations of helium blimps and balloons and the warning that heavier-than-air flight was not possible at this time.

Now here is an odd phenomenon: I remember pretty well almost every novel I've ever read. I remember Spillane's Mike Hammer shooting a beautiful naked woman in the belly so that she would die slowly. I remember thinking that it would not really have been very dangerous for James Bond to have had to crawl through a tunnel full of tarantulas. But aside from the aircraft, I remember nothing at all from the Encyclopedia Brittanica. When I read for information I do not retain the knowledge.

Leaving that particular town I had to leave the encyclopedia behind, as well as several other books, which, fortunately, were all paperbacks. It felt entirely appropriate to throw away *A Canticle for Leibowitz*, by Walter Miller, even though I had enjoyed it immensely. (I wish now that I had known about libraries.)

In general women are intelligent and generous. A woman gave me James Baldwin's *Go Tell It On the Mountain*, at the same time I had come across *Spoon River Anthology*, by Edgar Lee Masters. How excellent to compare them. It took twenty more years to stumble across Richard Wright's *Native Son*.

I also cannot remember why it seemed necessary to me to discard books after reading them. I owned a big roomy 1949 Chrysler so I could have filled the trunk with books. It may be that because I retain the knowledge, I carry the story, I have not felt the need for the book. The story has happened; one moves on.

Always the last to confess it, my memory is in fact weirdly selective and inventive. (That general phenomenon is the curse and genius of books—you can always be found out, you can always go back and check.) For years I'd been telling people about an excellent essay by Calvino called, "Why Read the Classics?" It does not say what I remember it saying. It's another essay in another Calvino book I've been remembering.

It may be that paperback books look like they should be discarded. The covers are famously trashy, such as a paperback of Anton Chekov short stories that had an illustration of a blond woman with her red dress half off. They begin to fall off apart after one reading. I have the nasty habit, and have carried it over to hardback books, of breaking the spine every time I turn a page so that the book will lie flat while I'm reading at the breakfast table. Books to me were just containers for stories, like wine bottles. The value was more or less exactly two dollars and forty-nine cents.

In Geneva in the late 60s and early 70s my rather large apartment had no bookshelf at all, even though by that time I had three dictionaries, which I read every day. Africans who were in town because of the international organizations (the working part of the United Nations is in Geneva, not New York) would often stay at my place, as would Indians from South America. They usually had paperback books. By that method I discovered Frantz Fanon, Georges Simenon, Simone de Beauvoir, Eduardo Galeano, Vladimir Lenin, Baruch Spinoza, José Ortega y Gasset, Jean Genet, and Federico García Lorca. My reading was not only without direction—it depended on friends. Beginning in the late 50s and continuing today, I have read at least three books a week, often as many as seven. (I've never had a television.) All read and discarded. In 1974 I was mostly on the Pine Ridge Reservation in South Dakota, mostly not reading at all except for obscene literature, such as the Rapid City newspapers.

Then I moved to New York. Book heaven. Readers' heaven. There was a shoe store in West Greenwich Village, which proclaimed that Susan Sontag bought her shoes there. No one had yet given me a book of hers but I knew the name from reading the *New Yorker* (when the price of that magazine went up to fifty cents I stopped buying it for awhile) and the *International Herald Tribune*. I had learned in Texas from a guy who was really a 'card-carrying communist' (he showed me his card!) to read the *Manchester Guardian* but it was not usually available.

It is not difficult to see why, but in New York my friends were mostly Indians, blacks, or Jewish guys. The Jewish guys all had small apartments, like mine, but stuffed with books—with paperback books wall-to-wall and floor-to-ceiling. They were all happy to loan me books, even though I was surly. It seemed pretentious to keep all that garbage. Just to show off how much you had read, I thought. I still did not have a bookshelf.

There were so many good bookstores but I would go in to look only briefly once in awhile. Row after row of books with no recommendations. If I remember correctly the *New Yorker* did not review books which had 'gone to paper' in those days and I could afford nothing else. It was not really productive to go from row to row and randomly choose books that seemed interesting—there were too many to choose from.

I had begun reading, in the military, as I said, as a way to escape my fellow thugs. The authors, the poets also, were not real to me. It was probably a gradual development, but maybe it began with Fanon. Maybe it began with sympathy, in other words, the feeling that I was talking with someone while reading.

There is a most excellent phrase, "she introduced me to...," Gerard Manley Hopkins or Calvino or some other writer. That there is a real human being who might speak to me, who I might know. Books and reading became social acts instead of a private escape from the world. A way to enter a larger world. What good luck to enter this community as an equal; that is, as an interested party, instead of for a purpose, education, for example. I've never read for instruction. It has also given me space to move, I hope. I often pretend to have read more than I have and at other times to have read less; if at a dinner someone says, "Oh, so you are following Adorno's analysis...," I'm willing to say that I've not read Adorno just to keep the conversation on a subject instead of degenerating into academic chatter.

It is the economy of paperback books that has allowed me to enter this community that is eternally on the road. I lived in New York for twelve years; longer than I've lived anywhere else. In 1987 I moved to Mexico. Even the cheapest paperbacks in Mexico were beyond the reach of us ordinary poor people. All over the Hispanic world books are too expensive for those who are to me 'ordinary' people. It means that a young person from a working class background in Mexico cannot have the privilege I've had because it is tied to money.

On the other side, after fifty years of wildly eclectic (but circumscribed by what is easily available) reading, I now see reading, being 'well-read,' as the same as other areas of social life. Literacy is not a necessity; sociality is the necessity.

My life in New York and earlier was greatly fortunate in the easy availability of cheap books. Now they are expensive everywhere. A typical paperback now costs about ten bucks, 20 if it is a book of 'quality.' In Mexico I had a bookshelf. I had begun, on a trip to Peru, to buy dictionaries of indigenous languages. Then in New York I began to have other books that I began to see as reference books. All of this amounted to not much, and neither did it weigh me down. Most paperbacks were still printed on paper instead of the strange and heavy plastic pages of today. But we took in an injured street dog who chewed up everything on the two bottom shelves.

Back in Europe for the past twenty years: Dublin, Brussels, Marseilles, Berlin, Rome, Naples, with long stops in Lisbon, Stockholm, Lille, Tours, Venice, Milan; I now think about how I might begin a library of 'the classics'—England, France, Spain, Germany, Russia, do not really have this beautifully broad and liberal bunch of writers. One must lean towards a field; philosophy, novels, etc., and even then it is contentious. Following Aby Warburg and my own peregrinations I think I won't build anything (except another bookshelf), just let a few interesting books freely associate.

Might I do this on my new laptop computer? It seems not. I now read Google and Wikipedia the way I once read dictionaries. The way I once read *Encyclopedia Britannica*. Nothing that I read there stays in my mind—except that most salamanders have neither gills nor lungs—such a disturbing fact is difficult to forget.

Jimmie Durham is an American-born sculptor, essayist, and poet, currently living in Europe.

Gitanjali Dang

The Physical Impossibility of Death in the Mind of Someone Moving

In Patrick Süskind's short story "Depth Wish" (1997), a young painter takes a review of her recent exhibition too much to heart. She is particularly transfixed by the reviewer's suggestion that she is lacking in her understanding of depth. It obsesses her to no end. Obsesses her right to the end, as it were.

The scenario presented by Süskind is far from the norm. To begin with, critics have little muscle. Furthermore, while the artist in Süskind's story becomes excessively preoccupied with depth, the art industry today is primarily lorded over by surface, and the shiny happy visibility that bounces off of it. The nomadic proclivities of contemporary art are in constant conspiracy with said visibility, thus making this aggressive strain of capitalist globalism the ultimate arbiter of visibility.

The noun nomad is bandied about expressly in contemporary art settings; however, its connotations are rarely explored in full. The white noise of jet propellers and the ambient music in waiting lounges mask certain predatory tendencies that are innate to this breed of nomads. Traditionally, nomadic cultures have three principal thrusts: hunter-gatherers, pastoral nomads, and peripatetic nomads.

Art is, without doubt, an industry of hunter-gatherers.

Human beings have been hunter-gatherers since the prehistoric era; it put food in the belly before the arrival of agrarian societies. Although it might seem that traditional nomadism of the sort is rare today, a quick scan reveals that this specific culture of nomadism is ingrained in our genotype.

We are forever chasing our own private El Dorados. The blame for this is perennially presumed to lie elsewhere. It is oftentimes pushed onto the likes of those unabashed hunter-gatherers who stalk malls and seek their nourishment in its glitter. In reality, though, the blame lies everywhere, albeit to varying degrees.

Contemporary art is particularly dexterous at this notorious skill of blame pushing. Needless to say, it is not above such relentless consumerism. Market, museum, artist, theorist, curator, critic, gallerist, and what have you, are captivated by hunting-gathering, which invariably covets the iconic or the ultra visible. Thus far, iconophilia has proven unerasable, even when the icon, read Willem de Kooning, has been decidedly erased.

Art's reliance on this subsistence method is inescapable because the industry is ruled by mobility—geographical, social, and everything else in between. Typically, this movement, both literally and metaphorically, is in search of greener pastures where the hunt is gamier. Within art, auctions probably qualify as the height of such nomadism. Auction houses ferret icons and gather them for the benefit of collectors, who then perform their own variation of the long-cherished routine.

Perpetual motion is important if art practitioners are to fish about like rapacious sharks. In order to have water, subsequently oxygen, wash through their gills, sharks must keep moving. Cessation of motion equals cessation of breath. But, of course, motion in itself is not the cause of the predicament. Mozart preferred composing in the back of a carriage and Goethe preferred the horseback. Closer to now, Saskia Sassen prefers to write when she's flying, and Haruki Murakami, a long-distance runner, has written extensively about his experiences in his memoir *What I Talk About When I Talk About Running* (2007). Murakami writes,

> For me, running is both exercise and a metaphor. Running day after day, piling up the races, bit by bit I raise the bar, and by clearing each level I elevate myself. At least

that's why I've put in the effort day after day: to raise my own level. I'm no great runner, by any means. I'm at ordinary—or perhaps more like mediocre—level. But that's not the point. The point is whether or not I improved over yesterday. In long-distance running the only opponent you have to beat is yourself, the way you used to be.[1]

The art industry's breakneck travels are in contravention with all that Murakami says and leaves unsaid. While Murakami tries with each run to push out of his comfort zone, the industry is keen on sinking deeper into the plushness of its comfort zones. Moreover, in demanding unremitting peripatetic extroversion from its players, the industry ensures that no mode of self or transportation will ever live up to its call for acceleration.

For individuals working within the parentheses of the business, failure to be on the move results in the severing of the visibility oxygen. Constant motion deceives members of the fraternity into mistakenly believing that they can parry the inevitable flat line forever: the physical impossibility of death in the mind of someone moving.

This movement also hampers the contemporariness in art. Giorgio Agamben writes,

> Contemporariness is, then, a singular relationship with one's own time, which adheres to it and, at the same time, keeps a distance from it. More precisely, it is that relationship with time that adheres to it through a disjunction and an anachronism. Those who coincide too well with the epoch, those who are perfectly tied to it in every respect, are not contemporaries, precisely because they do not manage to see it; they are not able to firmly hold their gaze on it.[2]

The contemporariness of contemporary art as we know it is oftentimes myopic in its attachment to the present. Its need for speed cancels room for introspection. As such, contemporary art is infrequently contemporary.

Contemporary art might not always be wholly contemporary but it rarely misses on an opportunity to be frenetically ironic; it is ironic even when it is trying to be anything but. Irony is contemporary art's big conceptual breakthrough. This droll irony is a corollary of slovenly contemporaneity.

In some cases, this irony is an attempt to assuage guilt regarding the high stakes of art; in most cases, however, industry insiders find it conveniently fashionable to covet it. Earlier this year, science discovered Quantum Stealth, a material that bends light around the wearer and makes them hidden. The ironic retort, as phrased by contemporary art, bends light around the artwork and in doing so makes its half-baked self-criticism and platitudes hidden. Little surprise then that Damien Hirst's *The Physical Impossibility of Death in the Mind of Someone Living*, a sculpture of a tiger shark in a formaldehyde-filled vitrine, is contemporary art at its most iconic, most ironic, and most hardcore.

Irony started off as an insider's patois, native to 20th century Euro-American territories. Christy Wampole, assistant professor of French at Princeton University, writes, "Ironic living is a first-world problem. For the relatively well educated and financially secure, irony functions as a kind of credit card you never have to pay back."[3]

The gradual opening up of economies in countries such as India and China was accompanied by, among other things, the seepage of irony from the first to the other worlds, the decentralization of collecting clout and the advent of intense mobility. Contemporary Indian art's globalization narrative is assertively signposted by each of the aforementioned.

Following her independence in 1947, India was committed to socialist agendas, which prioritized public ownership and controlled the entry of foreign goods into the country. In July 1991, after 44 years of being a closed protectionist economy, India opened up to neoliberal policies. In a bid to pull the nation out of a financial tight spot, Manmohan Singh—then finance minister; now prime minister—activated unprecedented economic changes, including deregulation and privatization.

Liberalization pried the Indian art market open and worked hugely in its favor. The boom time scenario translated into tremendous global and local attention. Suddenly, borders were porous. Indian art practitioners were crisscrossing skies and moving in and out of time zones. From education to exhibition displays; exponential infrastructure upgrade meant that everything was transformed. The groundbreaking information highway, which entered India around the same time, also added unparalleled fuel to the production of cultural capital. Access had never been so easy.

Liberalization ushered in new mediatic possibilities—including installation, site-specific work, video, and performance. Media which had previously been underused, or not used at all, were ushered in by artists such as Vivan Sundaram, Nalini Malani, Rummana Hussain, and Navjot. These and other artists from the 1970s and the 80s, mobilized non-traditional media—which did not enjoy a local market at the time—to distance themselves from capitalist globalism and to address the rise of communalism in a different visual idiom. On December 6, 1992, not long after the economic upheaval, came the demolition of the Babri Masjid, Ayodhya. The razing of the 16th century Mughal mosque—which believers hold as the birthplace of the Hindu deity Lord Rama—was followed by extended periods of communal turmoil.

On the other hand, if not at the other end of the spectrum, were the increasingly savvy artists, who came into their own in liberalized India. Artists such as Subodh Gupta, Atul Dodiya, Bharti Kher, and Jitish Kallat submerged themselves in explorations of uncharted territories of the self as anchored in a globalized world. Whilst the earlier generation saw themselves in relation to the society they inhabited, the younger bunch inverted the model and placed the artist at the center and made it so that everything emanated from there. A heightened subjectivity and a more zealous engagement, intended and unintended, with irony, were the hallmarks of their arrival.

Although the liberating effects of this newfangled nomadism enabled multi-polarity and helped smudge, to some degree, the Euro-

American axis of power, they also accelerated the arrival of full-blown icon-chasing nomadism in Indian art.

Indian art today is comfortable playing the circuit; its functionings are variously synchronized with those of its counterparts elsewhere; its reluctance to openly engage with commerce is a case in point. For instance, the art scene at large continues to identify itself as the 'art world' as opposed to the 'art industry.' Presumably because 'world' signifies a Romantic heroism, which is far more palatable than the assembly line connotations of 'industry.' This is where the defense mechanism of denial kicks in.

Denial is activated when one encounters facts so uncomfortable that rejecting their existence, in the face of all evidence to the contrary, appears like the best way out. While back-room gossip about art as luxury product has been documented sporadically, the denial helps keep up grandiose appearances.

Additionally, coming to terms with the denial would undoubtedly affect the industry's movements. In that, it will no longer be possible to partake of such high-octane nomadism with a sense of entitlement. Confronting denial and disturbing the status quo would also signify death.

The overwroughtness of the industry's doublespeak is such that while on the one hand it glorifies nomadism, on the other hand it is critical of those who indulge in it forthrightly. As such, an artist or a curator requesting to fly to their exhibition site on an air carrier of their choice, so they can rake in flying miles, is par for the course, not deviation from the course.

None of this is to imply that the art industry ought to be replaced by some Platonic construct. Far from being ugsome, the circuit and its nomadism are of critical importance. Having said that, the space populated by the industry also includes innumerable other networks—such as finance, architecture, biology, dentistry, cosmology, and agriculture. The industry is part of a larger, more complex system of networks, and no complex system can ever be stable. One such network includes individuals who are pushing for an aesthetic that is irony free and a nomadism that is less belligerent. This aesthetic project is distinct from the visual art project.

Visual art—called thus because its operative components rely either heavily or solely on visibility for their survival—requires that we constantly mind the gap between the artist and the art, the said and the unsaid, the done and the undone, the written and the unwritten. The aesthetic project, on the other hand, emerges from an embodied and consequently more irony-free practice, which keeps the gap to a minimum. In doing so, it ensures that light does not have to perform any physics-defying tricks. In lieu of bending light, embodied practices invite light to pass through their transparent prism and break into spectral colors.

In the aesthetic project you embody your aesthetic like a turtle embodies its home. Distinctions collapse, they become the same and you operate out of this sanctuary. Turtles are *khanabadosh*. A Hindustani word, *khanabadosh* stands for those who carry their homes with them. One could attempt to outwit the shark by deploying a decoy, a turtle. Implausible as it might sound, it is eminently possible for a turtle to give a shark an identity crisis. An amphibian, the turtle is part of two very different motionscapes. Despite this, its motion is contained, steady, and lacks pyrotechnics. Turtles and tortoises are slow in part because of the weight of their homes. The embodiment of home/aesthetic entails slowing down. Introversion, introspection, and sustainability are hard-wired into the embodied practice.

This in no way is to suggest that the visual art project and the aesthetic project don't intersect, because they do, and the results can be quite combustive when they do. Indian art practitioners such as artists Sheba Chhachhi, Valsan Koorma Kolleri, Abhishek Hazra, Kiran Subbaiah, Tejal Shah, Kausik Mukhopadhyay, and Nikhil Chopra are instances of such an intersection.

In September 2012, after some serious procrastination, this writer finally initiated Khanabadosh. An itinerant arts lab, Khanabadosh observes, as much as possible, the above-stated intersection paradigm. The delay in getting started had been caused mostly by the obstacle race better known as Bombay.[4] A city where space is nothing, if not, beleaguered. The lack of space was the big impasse en route to the intersection. In time, however, it (thankfully) came through that the space deadlock was just a regular prejudice. That it was possible to be, without being a space. A rush of gestalt accompanied the gradual eroding of this cul-de-sac. Soon after, Khanabadosh was inaugurated.

Thus far, the lab has undertaken three projects: *Ghar* by Javed Iqbal (September 2012), *Camouflage* by Valsan Koorma Kolleri (February 2013), and *Something to chew on* by Mona Gandhi (March 2013-ongoing).[5] Each of these artists is a Khanabadoshi and has undertaken an aesthetic project. Kolleri, as previously identified, is a committed holder of the intersection. An eminent Indian artist, Kolleri has been doggedly following an aesthetic project that took him away from production centers of Bombay and Delhi to the town of Thalassery on the Malabar Coast of Kerala. Here he works with local craftsmen to generate utilitarian objects like chairs and hopes that one day soon the monies yielded from this production outfit will enable him to set up an artists' center and residency. Significantly, Kolleri and other practitioners such as Shah and Chopra—who also recently shifted from Bombay to the more laid-back but very well-connected state of Goa—moved away from production centers following their arrival on the scene. Had they moved before creating a current of visibility, they would have, in all likelihood, been relegated to the backwaters.

A reporter and photojournalist, the Bombay-based Iqbal investigates and monitors displacement caused by the State-Maoist civil war being fought in pockets across the nation. Back home, when he's not reporting on this war, he tracks the displacement effected by ostensible slum rehabilitation projects incessantly ongoing in Bombay. Gandhi, a writer and media person, has been a raw foodist since May 2012. Her Khanabadosh project entails a monthly pay-what-you-want meal where Gandhi uncooks for a group of individuals and leads discussions on the politics and economics of food and nutrition.

Iqbal and Gandhi are outsiders to the exalted circuit. Be that as it may, it is entirely foreseeable that they will in time find themselves getting pulled into the fold. The overlaps between the aesthetic and the visual art projects are plenty and inevitable. Apropos to that: Although perpetrators of high capitalist globalism too have their life-support objects strapped on, they operate out of privilege and the velocity it engenders. Khanabadoshis don't mind living outside of the trap of the speedometer and through protracted periods of inactivity. This absence of doing is, in fact, the secret of their longevity.

These conflicting forces of making have always been around, with the perimeter perennially working towards slowing or destabilizing the clout of the overriding system. The marginalized vernacular of the aesthetic argument needs to be mobilized and centralized if we are to partialize the industry. This bringing-to-the-middle, however, is not without its pitfalls. Contemporary art's porosity is one its most salient features and, with time, aesthetic projects too are bound to get sucked into its swelling tide of iconophilia. The icon is everywhere. The icon is everything. The icon is unflappable.

Incidentally, icons have kinesis too. Velocity is the key to an icon's survival; a stationary icon is a dead icon. Failure to be on the move results in the severing of the visibility oxygen. Constant motion deceives icons into mistakenly believing that they can parry the inevitable flat line forever; the physical impossibility of death in the mind of someone moving.

Iconophilia might be inescapable but it is eminently possible to perform it in a less aggressive manner wherein hunting and gathering get replaced by looking and finding.

An identity crisis, then, might be just the thing for a behemoth that is all too self-assured. As the poet Theodore Roethke wrote, "Those who are willing to be vulnerable move among the mysteries." Far from vulnerable, the smug industry is only too eager to please. Now more than ever before, the circuit needs course-correction that will address the denial regarding its industry status.

While in the past these histories of patronages were discreet, present day bling has bestowed on them a blinding visibility. From Mughal emperors to residencies to biennials to not-for-profits, there's an urgent need for historiographical studies that inspect patronage genealogies across epochs and typologies. These histories need to be studied alongside the histories of modernities and such. These inquiries, in turn, should be conducted in tandem with a phalanx of aesthetic projects. Centering has its problems but it also activates visibilization, which is distinct from visibility in a manner reminiscent of the distinction between the aesthetic and the visual art projects.

We could take our cue from practices of visibilization that have made their impact through the recent revolutions and protests across the globe. In choosing to not be blinded by star-studded visibility, one could potentially activate the critical politics of visibilization and make apparent what has thus far been hushed up.

NOTES

1. Haruki Murakami, *What I Talk About When I Talk About Running*, translated by Philip Gabriel (London: Harvill Secker, 2007).
2. Giorgio Agamben, "What is the Contemporary?" in *What is an Apparatus? and Other Essays*, translated by David Kishik and Stefan Pedatella (Stanford, CA: Stanford University Press, 2009).

3. Christy Wampole, "How to Live Without Irony" in *The Stone, The New York Times* (November 17, 2012).

4. In 1995, the Hindu Right hectored the Bombay to Mumbai name-change into being. The renaming epidemic spreads unabated across the country. It is commonly recognized as a threat to the nation's multi-cultural heritage.

5. This essay was written in May 2013.

Gitanjali Dang is an independent curator, writer, and shapeshifter based out of Bombay. She has curated over twenty projects of contemporary art and in September 2012 she initiated the itinerant arts lab Khanabadosh. She is a research associate at Zurich University of the Arts' (ZHdK) Institute for Contemporary Art Research, IFCAR. Here she is working towards a project which broadly aims to connect global streets via a network of public art projects. She has lectured and presented papers at Jawaharlal Nehru University (JNU), Delhi; ZHdK, Zurich; Kunstmuseum Thun, Thun; and Goethe-Institut Bombay; among others. She has contributed essays to several exhibition catalogues and publications. Gitanjali's criticism and articles on the arts and culture at large have appeared in leading local and international publications including *Art Papers*, *frieze* and *Art-Agenda*.

Niels Van Tomme

The Trouble with the Migrant Metaphor

In this text I would like to address the contemporary appearance of the figure of the migrant, in particular as a generative counterpoint to our celebration of the so-called new nomadic lifestyle, two modes of experience that have often been collapsed in contemporary discourse. If this lifestyle is characterized by a relentless passing through diverse social, cultural, economic, and geographic spheres, then the migrant—despite its transitory identity—should be seen as a static figure; being relocated from her home, she is importantly excluded from the cosmopolitan freedom of movement that distinctly defines the former state. Hers is precisely a life, not a lifestyle, determined by a totalizing existential disruption instead of the privilege of a free choice. According to Slovenian philosopher Slavoj Žižek, it is too easy "to praise the hybridity of the postmodern migrant subject, no longer attached to specific ethnic roots," as for her this supposed hybridity designates "a very tangible traumatic experience of never being able to settle down properly, […] an experience full of anxiety, and demanding great effort, […] a traumatic shock which destabilizes [her] entire existence."[1]

A similar conceptual discrepancy can be found in today's contemporary art world, namely through its equation of the underprivileged migrant worker with the internationally traveling art worker (literally translated in discourses related to the artist as migrant, such as curator Katja Kobolt's statement that "both artist […] and migrant embody the capacity of translating personal, social, and political experience, and both […] are believed to function in a way which transcends national borders").[2] This gesture is all too often emphasized when the art community seeks to highlight its supposed flexible, dynamic, and ever-changing transnational nature, an idea which has prompted the writing of this text. To be clear, the art worker should be understood here not so much as the individual artist or curator but as a vastly expanding international network of artists and curators who move freely between residencies, biennials, academies, and other professional frameworks.

Beyond evoking the problematic nature of the above-mentioned one-dimensional equation, the question remains how one can critically approach the realness of such a vast and ungraspable subject matter as migration through the realm of contemporary artistic practices. I wish to evoke two artworks here, which reflect critically upon the migrant condition, while playfully negotiating the topic of migration. They do so through a complex interplay of experience and research, critical conceptual thought, and aesthetic mediation. Constructing a critical thought process about migration, these artworks show that there is a distinct divide between the migrant and artist subject, two states of being which cannot constructively be equated with one another, but which can be thoughtfully explored through artistic practices.

Immigrant Song

The Immigrant Song, 2008, shows a headshot of Bosnian artist Damir Nikšić, endlessly singing:

> *I say: I'm here because I want to be here*
> *And you say: No you're here because we let you be here*
> *And I say: I'm here because I choose to be here*
> *And you say: No you're here because we let you be here*

As the video progresses, Nikšić, who was at the time of production a recent immigrant to Sweden, interprets each repetition with a slightly different intonation and singing style, notably showing exhaustion by the end, which renders the piece indisputably amusing but also discomforting and alienating, a feeling reinforced by the artist's head framed so intimately close. Through these strategies of estrangement, *The Immigrant Song* questions its own mode of address, and makes one wonder whether it really represents the exceptional status of the contemporary migrant subject, as its title suggests, or whether there might be something altogether different at stake.

If the video is indeed a comment on the paradoxical nature of the migrant subject (the "choice" to be here vs. being allowed to be here), it reflects foremost the freedom of movement as well as the possibility and impossibility of personal choice. In that case, *The Immigrant Song* only talks about voluntary migration, considering that the subject the artist gives voice to indeed *wants to be here*. However, such one-dimensional interpretation ultimately means that a huge number of migrants who are forced to leave their home countries because of political, economic, or other life-threatening conditions—involuntary displaced—is excluded from Damir Nikšić's meditation, as the video doesn't seem to address the ones who *don't necessarily want but need to be here*. In this light, it is interesting to read the following quote by Nikšić from an interview I conducted with him in 2009:

> There's an entire population that is marginalized and excluded from many state-supported cultural events, financed by the taxpayer's money. [...] I'm talking about immigrants and other minorities. We don't see them represented in museums of contemporary art. We might even laugh at that idea. Their problems and their voices are absent.[3]

Of course, relating the work back to a merely one-sided reflection on the topic of migration would be an act of intentional misreading. Making use of the migrant metaphor, *The Immigrant Song* allows the artist to relate complex issues of in- and exclusion of the migrant to the very status of the artwork when it is exhibited in a gallery space. Not unlike Damir Nikšić's migrant who *is here because he wants to be here* while simultaneously being *here because we let him be here*, artworks in an exhibition are present despite their paradoxical ontological status, the "we," in that case, referring to the institutionalized conditions that allow for their appearance.

Foreigners Everywhere

Foreigners Everywhere is the statement that Claire Fontaine has been duplicating in neon since 2005, in a wide diversity of languages, except, importantly, English. As the piece gets most often displayed behind gallery windows facing a street, the sign creates a somewhat antagonistic relationship with its locality, interjecting the surrounding public space with a foreign language, acting out the immigrant's often-assumed status as intruder and unwelcomed subject. During Claire Fontaine's solo exhibition at the Aspen Art Museum in Aspen, Colorado, in 2009, the phrase was translated in Ute, a Native American language. Installed above the entrance of the museum, the neon projected a light on the woods surrounding its site, metaphorically connecting the phrase, and its message, with the land on which it was displayed. This particular version of *Foreigners Everywhere*, and the language which it employs, points to the period when Native Americans were the only inhabitants of the area, the times before colonization.

In this way, Claire Fontaine reflect on some of the more disturbing aspects of historical processes and their role in shifting the perspective about migration, while simultaneously calling for an empathic affiliation with an adversary political subject—the migrant. As the artists have noted, "they have told 'go back home' to people who have lost their homes so many times that [these people] have accepted going to look for it on the other side of the world."[4] Since the United States has been populated by a long-term flow of immigrants, while in reality this implied the annihilation of its native population, Claire Fontaine's dictum that "foreigners are not those who come from elsewhere" becomes particularly significant in a U.S. context.[5]

Seen as such, the statement "Foreigners Everywhere" makes clear that "foreigner" is an incessantly reversible concept. The ambivalent nature of these words gets intersected within the different sites and contexts where the neon signs are installed. In a sense, it stresses a duality: the fact that we will always find foreigners wherever we go, but also that we will be foreigners in every place we go to. To quote Claire Fontaine once again: "The translations of the two words act as subtitles to public and private spaces, awakening dormant antagonisms and fears." Framed this way, the work relates to what Svetlana Boym has called the "art of everyday dissent," a form of art that uses the device of estrangement "connected to the embarrassment about identity."[6] According to Boym, the migrant's "multilingual consciousness is frequently described as a complex mental geography that is hidden from view."[7] Claire Fontaine, through this series of signs and their particular use of linguistic expression, make precisely such exilic sentiments painfully visible, using alienation and antagonism as the migrant's somewhat devious, albeit preferred, form of aesthetic expression.

New possibilities

Migrants who are thrown into an uncertain and unpredictable future experience the above-discussed issues, as explored indirectly in the works by Damir Nikšić and Claire Fontaine, on a day-to-day basis. For them this is not about an aesthetic understanding, but the reality of their daily life. The broader question I would like to address is how such radical experiences of exclusion (Damir Nikšić) and antagonism (Claire Fontaine) can relate to the new nomadic lifestyle of art workers who often refer to the migrant paradigm—and its supposed "hybridity," as quoted earlier by Žižek—as a prerequisite for their own lives. How can one possibly conceptually link such alienating and incompatible existential condition when one's lifestyle depends on the smooth global flow of cultural capital and artistic exchange? And in which way can a new emerging class of international art workers relate oneself to another developing class of permanent migrant workers, if their fundamental subjective experience depends on in-, rather than exclusion?

Exile is much more appealing as a metaphor than it is as an existential experience. When, in early 2011, in the wake of the political unrests in the Middle East and North Africa, the Mediterranean island of Lampedusa was overflown by a steady influx of migrants, the island was forced to open up the gates of its detention center to accommodate these large groups of people. As a result, all of Lampedusa became a migrant camp. Some of the local inhabitants opened the Museum of the Immigrants, for which they scraped together the 400 euros in monthly rent themselves:

> It's not much more than a windowless room with a stone floor, but it's full of boards: a comb, a pot, an ashtray, a telephone book, a mirror, a single sneaker, Korans and Bibles. "These aren't just objects," says D'Ancona [an inhabitant of the island], "[t]hey're clues that tell us something about people's dreams." She and a few friends found many of the objects on the beach [...], others are items that less fortunate refugees were carrying with them when they died.[8]

The institutional structure of the blooming autonomous well-funded spaces of 21st century artistic production—its numerous museums, artist-in-residence programs, biennials, schools, exhibition spaces, research centers, etc.—could not be farther removed from the real spaces that migrants, such as those on Lampedusa inhabit. If the global art worker really wants to connect to the struggle of migrants worldwide, she shouldn't attempt to establish tenuous links between these disparate worlds, an impossibly unattainable act, as I have explored, but find novel ways of joining the fight against the injustices these people inevitably face. For the artist and curator hold unique positions from which they can creatively propose new possibilities of equality, social justice, and consciousness from within the aesthetic domain.

NOTES

1. Slavoj Žižek, *The Ticklish Subject: the Absent Centre of Political Ontology* (New York: Verso, 2008, first edition 1999), 220-221.
2. Katja Kobolt, "Art and Migration - The Troubled Relations between the Centre and the Periphery," http://http://www.kitch.si/livingonaborder/node/41, accessed October 23, 2012.
3. Damir Nikšić quoted in Niels Van Tomme, "The European Loser," *Foreign Policy in Focus* (August 27, 2009), http://www.fpif.org/articles/the_european_loser, accessed Oct 23, 2012.
4. Claire Fontaine, 'Foreigners Everywhere,' in *Micro-Historias y Macro-Mundos*, ed. Magalí Arriola and Magnolia de la Graza (Mexico City: Instituto de Nacional de Belles Artes, 2010), 87.
5. Lieven Decauter, 'The Permanent Catastrophe,' in *The Capsular Civilization: On the City in the Age of Fear*, (Rotterdam: NAi Publishers, 2004), 99; and Claire Fontaine, 88.
6. Svetlana Boym, *The Future of Nostalgia*, (New York: Basic Books, 2001), 291.
7. Ibid., 256.
8. Katharina Peters, 'Finding Help, Hate, and Hope on Lampedusa,' *Der Spiegel* (February 17, 2011), http://www.spiegel.de/international/world/an-influx-of-refugees-finding-help-hate-and-hope-on-lampedusa-a-746156.html, accessed October 23, 2012.

Niels Van Tomme is a New York-based curator, researcher, and critic. Most recently, he curated the travelling exhibition *Where Do We Migrate To?* (Baltimore, New York, New Orleans, Karlstad), as well as the group exhibitions *Melancholy is not enough...* (Bucharest) and *There is Nothing There* (New York). He is a Contributing Editor of *ART PAPERS* and publishes internationally in journals, magazines, and exhibition catalogues. Van Tomme has been a guest critic at M.I.T. (Cambridge), Parsons The New School for Design (New York), and Vassar College (Poughkeepsie), among others. He currently works as Visiting Curator at the Center for Art, Design and Visual Culture in Baltimore where his project *Visibility Machines: Harun Farocki & Trevor Paglen* will open in the fall of 2013.

Melissa Chiu

Reflections on Curating Asian Art

At no other time in our history has it been so easy to travel across countries and continents. For some, this has meant working and living in different cities, or even countries, a phenomenon largely driven by economics and the search for employment. This has caused deep cultural changes, which are yet to be fully understood. For art this has meant a greater sense of communication across and amongst cultures—creating a very different work dynamic for artists and curators. Where once it was an imperative for successful artists to travel and settle in art centers such as Paris or New York—think of Yoko Ono or Yayoi Kusama who were in New York in the 1960s. This changed toward the late 90s when the art world became interested in art created outside these "centers"—perhaps an after-effect of multicultural politics earlier in the decade—and artists who lived outside centers were sought after for inclusion in international exhibitions and biennials, which became the main form of circulation for many of their works. This was the time when the careers of William Kentridge from South Africa, Cai Guo-Qiang who had just relocated from China to Japan to New York, and Kimsooja from South Korea were launched in exhibitions in São Paulo, Shanghai, and Sydney. It seemed, at the time at least, as if the art world had opened up to a much greater potential—where artists outside Europe and the United States could make a statement with an international impact. This would have been unthinkable the decade before.

Now, if we think of the dawn of the 21st century, what has the real impact of this new global thinking been? Where once, curators only had to familiarize themselves with the artistic developments of Europe and America, there is certainly an expectation that they understand developments in Latin America, Africa, and Asia. Yet one of the bigger questions we must ask is how if at all has it changed curatorial practices or even the way we think of art history? One could argue that the curatorial processes and rationale, as well as the type of exhibitions, has not changed greatly in the past 20 years although there have been some exceptional breakthroughs. At the time of writing, both MoMA and the Guggenheim Museum are holding exhibitions of Japanese post-War avant-garde art. While both efforts are historical appraisals of knowledge already sifted through academic research, it signals a new level of interest by major American museums in art that lies beyond their usual focus on Euro-American art. Both exhibitions distill art historical research through the project of reprising an art movement in Asia for the art historical canon.

This coincidental programing at two significant New York museums draws on 20 years of large-scale introductory exhibitions of Asian art. The curatorship of Asian art in the United States began in the mid-90s with national survey exhibitions of thematic pan-Asian art such as *Traditions/Tensions: Contemporary Art in Asia* organized by Asia Society in 1996, but more often than not the organizing principle was in terms of the nation-state whether it was Japanese, Chinese, Indian, or even Pakistani art.[1] These ideas became more refined into monographic exhibitions as artists in Asia developed a body of work that allowed an in-depth survey. This could be identified as a second phase of curatorship and treatment of Asian contemporary art—an interest in individual artists and their artistic development. We saw this in the treatment of Montien Boonma and Zhang Huan at the Asia

Society as well as Lee Ufan and Cai Guo-Qiang at the Guggenheim Museum or, more recently, Ai Weiwei at the Mori Art Museum in Tokyo and Zarina Hashmi at the Hammer Museum in Los Angeles. This shift from the artist as a national representative to an individual is a significant one because it starts to make an argument for the treatment of artists from Asia as creators rather than as symbols of geo-political shifts that are sometimes the meta-narrative of such exhibitions. The third phase, the one we are currently witnessing, is an interest in the 20th century, especially the identification of art movements that stand parallel to the existing canon arguing for a revised and more inclusive art history. Examples include the Japanese post-war period with *Gutai: Splendid Playground* (2013) at the Guggenheim Museum and *Tokyo 1955—1970: A New Avant-Garde* (2012) at the Museum of Modern Art along with *Art and China's Revolution* exhibition in 2008 and the *Iran Modern* exhibition in 2013, both at Asia Society. These three curatorial treatments reveal a tendency from the general to the specific with a certain progressive logic. So what is the result of this new sense of internationalism for curators and ultimately museums? Does it truly change art history with the addition of artists and art works that would never have otherwise been considered, or do they remain footnotes to a canon maintained in the West? Furthermore, do these exhibitions and the surrounding scholarship encourage a superficial leveling out or conflation of significant local differences in favor of universal values? Has it created a body of knowledge that alters the way that art history will be chronicled? These are all questions that remain to be answered but one hopes that the changes that have been observed in the past 20 years taking place in museums and ultimately curatorial practice are irrevocable rather than a passing trend that may be reversed at any time.

* * *

These issues are for the field to determine and we see strides made in more complex approaches and responses to these challenges, especially as we see more graduate students embark on research, curators enter the newly founded museums, and of course artists emerge on the international art scene. Where once the entire idea of Asian contemporary art as a field was questioned, today it is considered a critical part of a complex global art world. As a region with over 30 countries and just as many languages and dialects, shared spiritual beliefs yet separate national founding narratives, the development of contemporary art in Asia is a remarkable phenomenon of the 20th century. If I reflect on a more personal level, of what I encountered as a curator in Asia in the early 90s, one of the main issues was the difficulty of communication and access to information. It was a time when email was not in usage so communicating with artists wasn't possible since many did not even have access to a telephone landline. This made travel even more essential—and for longer periods of time. The research really began when you landed in the city. There were few books and the Internet hadn't developed. The art world in these cities such as Beijing, Hanoi, Tokyo, and even Singapore was also much smaller so you could connect with the key figures in the art world there. It was an art world of artists. There were few curators working in the region and there were no museums or arts infrastructure in these countries with perhaps the exception of South Korea and Japan. This led to the development of artist spaces, which grew in importance as significant repositories of knowledge and the only places for artists to exhibit their work. Examples included IT Park in Taipei, Command N in Tokyo, and Loop in Seoul.[2] In the 90s some countries also had strict rules about the exhibition of contemporary art in the public sphere with censorship being commonplace. This was particularly true of Vietnam and China where artists during this decade had to find ways around government and police surveillance and intervention.

One of the most significant curatorial issues of this period was a degree of dissent about representation—who was chosen to be curators from particular countries in the international circuit. At a time when few in the region spoke English, it was sometimes those with language skills or even those who had migrated to Europe who acquired important roles. Exhibitions such as *Transculture* curated at the Venice Biennale by Fumio Nanjo, based in Tokyo, in 1997 and the *Traditions/Tensions* exhibition in 1996 curated by Apinan Poshyananda, based in Bangkok, are examples of significant projects that defined a new global grammar for curatorial practice. What the work of the Asia-Pacific Triennial in Australia, begun in 1993, did to develop curatorial talent during this period is also notable. At the same time that curators in the region were developing a curatorial voice, curators in Europe and the U.S. began to demonstrate interest. Criticism was leveled at these curators who sometimes "parachuted" for a few days into Asian cities with a charge to select a couple of works for an international exhibition with little local knowledge and understanding of the historical or cultural context in which the art was being produced. The issue at play was often a disconnect between the local art scene and international interests.[3] To some extent this has been offset by the development of curators living in Asia who have begun to play a more active international role. There are also curators from the U.S. and Europe who have chosen to dedicate longer periods in-country to familiarize themselves with the local culture, history, and societal dynamics. The impact of this is a more informed understanding of the environment where the art work is produced. This has always been one of the complexities of presenting Asian art—all too often there are incorrect assumptions made about its lineage, influences, and reference points. One example is the Political Pop movement in China that developed in the early 90s. The images of Mao and references to everyday popular culture led many to draw references to American Pop Art, yet the real influence on these artists was the preceding period of the Cultural Revolution (1966-1976) from which many of the images were derived. With more local information we are able to avoid drawing conclusions from our own knowledge-base. So spending more time getting to know the cultural context is now a curatorial imperative—it affords an expansion of experiences and knowledge.

Today the two developments that have had the greatest impact on artists and curators in Asia have been that of museum-building, both public and private, and the emergence of the market. This has provided for a greater number of opportunities to organize exhibitions and show art works while the market has offered some degree of financial support for artists. These have made the art scene across Asia more robust with a varied art ecology yet there are cautions we need to be aware of. Is the fast-growing number of museums sustainable? And is the number of art fairs and auctions, as well as the discussion and ranking of artists in terms of sales, a truly valid way to judge art? These questions are no less relevant to a broader consideration of developments in the international contemporary art world, signaling that Asia, once considered very much a separate region with its own conditions and concerns, is now linked and interconnected with developments around the world. This is also the case for curators, where once curators only felt compelled to learn about art in America and Europe, now there is an expectation that they are informed and knowledgeable about developments around the world, including Asia.

NOTES

1. See for example, Alexandra Munroe (ed.), *Japanese Art After 1945: Scream Against the Sky* (exhibition catalogue), Guggenheim Museum: New York, 1996; Minglu Gao, *Inside Out: New Chinese Art* (exhibition catalogue), Asia Society: New York, 1998; Jane Farver (ed.), *Out of India: Contemporary Art of the South Asian Diaspora* (exhibition catalogue), Queens Museum of Art: New York.
2. A useful guide to the alternative spaces in Asia is Yasuko Furuichi (ed.), *Alternatives: Contemporary Art Spaces in Asia* (Tokyo: The Japan Foundation Asia Center, 2001).
3. For a discussion of some of the issues at play, see Joan Kee, "Trouble in New Utopia," *positions: east asia cultures critique* 12.3 (2004), 667-686.

Dr. Melissa Chiu is Director of the Asia Society Museum and Senior Vice President for its Global Arts and Cultural Programs. Previously, she was Founding Director of the Asia-Australia Arts Centre in Sydney, Australia (1996-2001). As a leading authority on Asian contemporary art, she has guided a number of major initiatives at the Asia Society Museum, including founding and establishing Asian Contemporary Art Week, a city-wide event begun under her direction in 2002; the launch of a contemporary art collection focused on video art and photography to complement the museum's outstanding Rockefeller Collection of traditional Asian art. Dr. Chiu has curated nearly 30 exhibitions of international art including projects with Shirin Neshat, Cai Guo-Qiang, Zhang Huan, and Yoshitomo Nara. Her scholarly contributions include editor, Asian contemporary art and Asian American art chapters for Oxford Art Online, and is the author and editor of several books, monographs, and anthologies, such as *Breakout: Chinese Art Outside China* (Charta); the first-ever introductory books on the topic of Asian contemporary art, *Asian Art Now* (Monacelli Press), *Contemporary Asian Art* (Thames and Hudson), and an anthology of collected writings *Contemporary Art in Asia: A Critical Reader* (MIT Press).

Yannis Ziogas

Risk and Danger: Six incidents of a nomadic process. The paradigm of Visual March to Prespes.

According to Urlich Beck,[1] danger in traditional societies was personal and individual, it was a phenomenon that could be understood instantly and would be perceived immediately since it was visible. On the contrary, in contemporary societies, danger has become unpredictable, invisible, and "democratic" since it does not appear in parts of the population but in the entire population regardless of privileges and positions.[2] In a nomadic process the individual establishes a condition that reveals many of the archetypal characteristics often lost in the contemporary context. The nomadic process is a condition when the body is moving itself into places for a need of finding refuge, food, settlement.

In a nomadic process related to an artistic activity, danger and risk are involved. In an artistic activity the need that initiates the process is the search for territories of artistic experience and practice that have not yet been explored. It is also the quest for a new relationship between the body of the artist and the environment.

A nomadic process can initiate ways that establish the relationship of the artist to society in three ways. The first is the relationship of every individual artist to his/her body. The body is perceived as a society with its own rules and possibilities.[3] The second is his/her relationship to other artists who participate in the activity. The third is the relationship of traveling artistic nomads to the societies they meet along the way of traveling.

Several incidents from the nomadic project *Visual March to Prespes*[4] will be presented here to illustrate the way physical danger activates a conceptual risk. The project has been realized over the past seven years in Prespes, Greece, which lies at the northern border of Greece. Visual March to Prespes is a process in which art students, artists, and theoreticians are involved in discovering and examining the landscape of Prespes. The outcome of the process (artworks, essays, or simply short texts) reflects the energy of the process.

The following incidents were selected as illustrations of the way danger shapes reality during the *Visual March to Prespes* process. The various qualities of risk that are described in these incidents allow the individuals who participated in the process to shape a spiritual status that transforms his/her relationship both to the environment (external transformation) but also to him/herself and especially to his/her body.

An important part of *Visual March to Prespes* is the relationship of the body to the environment the way the body discovers, reflects, shapes, and has been shaped by the landscape. The landscape in this case is not only an environmental entity, but primarily a field, even in the traditional use of the art term. In that landscape/field, weather phenomena, incidents, fatigue, even pain, create the experience of the individual and of the group where he/she participates. Danger is a significant part of that process since it is one of the main factors that shapes the process. In a nomadic process, danger is constantly present on many levels and characteristics: the difficulty of the terrain, the physical limitations of the individual and the group, injuries, weather conditions, ammunition remaining from past wars (bombs, grenades), and the constant invisible presence of animals that can attack. Danger allows people to see their limitations and either try to move beyond them or accept them and stay in their current status.

In a nomadic process the concept of incident is perhaps the defining characteristic: the process (no matter how well planned it is) will be defined from the unexpected episodes that will appear: all of a sudden an object will appear along the way, another person will pass through during an itinerary, a snake will cross our path, a thunderstorm will erupt. These incidents are the episodes that shape a process of nomadic character. The accidental meetings allow the interpretation of the traces beyond the stereotypes or the predefined plans. The artist becomes in that way a collector of incidents.

The incidents of the *Visual March to Prespes* process can be separated between those that are related to an actuality and those related to the way the individual interprets reality. They are all characterized from the contrast between a sense of paradise that the landscape environment provides and the hidden stories that are widespread. The main danger of the process was the option of changing identity: working in a nomadic process is removing oneself from previous certainties. The following incidents describe moments when the individual identity of the nomad/artist came into crisis.

Incident 1
The Fear of Artistic Practice
06/29/2007

The first day that we started *Visual March to Prespes* was a June morning in 2007. We were there at an altitude of 1,600m, a group of artists and students ready to start the first Visual March. It was a celebratory atmosphere of something new or at least something different. Ahead of us was a five-day hike where we would explore the landscape between Florina and Prespes. As I gazed at the group of my colleagues, happy for their (our) effort to support a new approach, I was simultaneously feeling, as an artist, the fear of the new: what are we trying to accomplish now? Who are we, what are we trying to initiate? We are nomads away from the predetermined art world in the middle of nowhere. There was nothing here from the well-established structures and art world hierarchies. Where are we, and for what reason are we going to discover anything at all, or is all of this just in vain? There was the quest of a new identity, an identity that would be far removed from who we are and what we stand for. I was not a mountaineer; I was not even in a good shape. Until then my art practice was object-oriented and all of a sudden I found myself at the beginning of a participatory process. I was staring at the mountains, the peaks ahead of us. We were not in an amusement process; we were artists in search of new practices. By removing ourselves from our ordinary milieu we were able to face challenges of artistic and personal identities. And, at least for myself, I felt afraid of that because I put myself in a situation of ongoing challenge. The mountains, the bad weather, the physical exhaustion were ahead of us but I was not sensing any danger from the difficulty of that effort. The danger was in the change of personal identity, of my art identity. The dangers that would occur will relate to that aspect of my individual reality and not to the reality of the natural landscape.

Incident 2
The Non-reality of Danger
06/07/2009

In the area of Prespes the weather can change swiftly and often does so dramatically. In one case while hiking in an area between two lakes, a huge thunderstorm erupted. It was right after sunset when the sky turned black and the tempest started abruptly. Thunderstorms started to cross the sky with strong repeated crashes. We felt totally unprotected, in a total condition of risk. We still had a couple of kilometers to cross until we reached the building that could host us. We kept running, wet from the rain and frightened by the seemingly apocalyptic explosions occurring above our heads. Kilometers of electric lines crossed the dark sky with constant explosive clashes. Then all of a sudden in the same violent way that it appeared, the tempest stopped. The sky started to become clear again. Eventually we learned that the reason there were so many thunderstorms was the placement of a huge rod that collects lightning from the entire area. What we experienced was an artificial danger that had nothing to do with any real threat but just with a controlled condition. The danger was artificial, it was not real—it was more or less a Walter de Maria *Lightning Field*. We thought that we were away from artificiality; however we were in the midst of a controlled environment of climatic changes.

Incident 3
The Trace of Danger
10/07/2009

One of the most imposing sites in the area of Prespes is the Kokalis Cave. The cave was the location for the hospital of the Democratic Army, the communist party during the Greek Civil War 1946-49. It is situated in a very narrow valley, invisible to airplanes. A photographer friend of mine wanted to record the place and we drove to the area, but since the road was very muddy we decided to walk. While we walked in the wet road we saw on the ground very clear footprints from an animal, obviously a bear. The area of Prespes is a protected area for bears and there are many in the vicinity. The danger was there. There was not just a single trace but a series of footprints indicating that a bear had walked there before us, just a few hours, a few minutes, maybe even a few seconds ago. Our dilemma: shall we keep walking or shall we return? I called another friend of mine, a very experienced mountaineer, who told us: "Keep walking and talk loud!" We followed his advice and we started talking loudly and following the bear's footprints. We were walking along an invisible companion or an invisible threat. For more than a kilometer we followed them and at a certain point the footprints left the road in the opposite direction of the cave. We were safe. The danger had left. For two kilometers we walked along the mark of danger, along potential disaster. The aim to reach the cave was as clear as the accompanying threat.

Incident 4
Changing Identities
06/05/2008

Many trails cross the woods. Some of them are the paths that were followed by immigrants in the 1990s and early 2000s to cross the border to reach Florina, the nearest city to the border. One can still see along these paths hundreds if not thousands of shoes and various pieces of clothing lying on the ground. One can see shoes ranging from the most ordinary shoes to high-heeled shoes, dispersed all over the area. These piles were developed along the trails that were the same trails used by the guerrillas in the Civil War and by the merchants of the Byzantine and Ottoman era. All these rags and rotten objects had Albanian inscriptions on them and coming across them is not only an acquaintance with a familiar object found in a strange place, but also crossing one world with another language and alphabet. What are these clothes about, why are they left here? The immigrants (men, women, and children), after days and nights of walking and hiding in the mountains, arrived at this area that is close to their final destination. But their ordinary clothes, not fancy hiking equipment, were already dirty and tattered. So they would discard them and change into clean attire that had been well protected in plastic bags. These nomads threw away their former identity in order to be dressed in a new identity and be as safe as they thought they could be in the new environment when they arrived. By removing their former clothes, they were removing the danger of being the other, the enemy, or, at least, the alien, and transforming themselves into the familiar.

Incident 5

The Imminent Danger

06/30/2012

A group of participants in the *Visual March* were hiking in the midst of the woods when we came across a red and white stripped band surrounding an area of the woods. The band, a most explicit symbol of danger, was wrapped around more than a kilometer of the beautiful green area. The red/green complementary color relationship created an almost aesthetically beautiful scene. A symbol of an imminent terror in the midst of sublimity: a forbidden forest. We kept walking along our path outside the forbidden area and then we saw the reason for this restriction: a military unit of minesweepers of about 30 soldiers was cleaning the area of mines 50 years after the end of the Greek Civil War. It was an awkward meeting: we, the traveling art-nomads with our colorful clothing and our relaxed approach met a group of soldiers with their uniforms, military vehicles, and weapons trying to remove terror. The forest was no longer innocent. It was neither sublime nor beautiful. The wounds were there. The danger was tangible. We were not walking in an area protected from its beauty rather we were exposed to the possibility of a mine explosion. The reality of the past was threatening us with whatever remained from the imminent presence of a long finished war. But is a war ever finished? History was real because it was dangerous.

Incident 6

The Presence of Death

06/28/2010

The area of Prespes was the theater of fierce battles during the civil wars. More than 300,000 soldiers, men, and women fought on either side for a number of years. Tens of thousands died. Many of them were not buried, or they were buried in haste. There are tales that mountaineers, even 20 years after the war, continued to find skeletons in the remote area. Meeting death is one of the risks in the *Visual March to Prespes*. Trenches, which are still visible, are the most probable places for such a meeting. These trenches were developed for many kilometers, cutting the mountains in slices. They have since been filled with dirt, however they are still visible. What is this dirt covering? What will these trenches reveal? Are they just graves? Who is buried under the dirt of the trenches? Every time we cross them we feel not only the pain of those who died there but also the sense that they are not trenches but actual cemeteries. The entire area is transformed into a cemetery of war and of the human hope for political and social change. Crossing a trench is like crossing a potential grave, meeting death in its more brutal illustration. And that is by itself a risk and a source of fear.

The mines, the bears, the high-heeled shoes, the clothes, the lightning rod, the bear prints, the red and white band, and the trenches all create incidents of danger, not only physical dangers but also the risk of changing one's identity. The incidents described are episodes of the imminent threat, of the danger that shapes identities and is part of the artistic nomadic process. They are related to identity in almost every aspect: identity as a collective process, individual identity, the way our body understands reality, and the way we interpret who we are. Danger allows us to move beyond the limitation of the profane and the established, and questions the essence of who we are, what we are doing, and for what reason. Nomadic processes such as the *Visual March to Prespes* emancipate these possibilities, offering in that way the option for an individual quest for identity.

These incidents, and the nomadic process that initiated them, have transformed my work process as an artist. As a visual artist, having worked over the years in large urban environments (Athens, New York, Chicago, Detroit) has created in me a mentality that was related to these places. My work was studio oriented; my references related to the urban environment, to the art world, my entire practice was connected to the notion of an artist with a base, a studio in a specific place, an art-activity situated in the city. Nomadic process and nature were to me distant frameworks and abstract concepts.

After 2006 when I started to work in Florina, teaching in an Art School, I found myself in a totally different environment and life process. On the one hand I had to travel between at least three cities (Florina, Athens, and Chalkis). On the other hand I introduced in my teaching a nomadic process: almost every other week my students and I traveled to different places of the area, absorbing what each place has to offer. I started to live nomadically, changing places almost every other day either as an individual artist or as an art teacher. Florina is situated next to Prespes and the *Visual March* activity that was initiated there has totally transformed my concept. From all the changing environment, I was most challenged by nature. The lessons that I taught myself being a nomad in nature has altered the way I experienced artistic practice and life in general.

Living in nature was different from anything I had known thus far. The experience of nomadic life in nature has allowed me to preserve my mental sobriety in the current harsh economic and political era. It was then that I discovered for the first time in my artistic life the importance of the body. Living nomadically, having to change the living environment so often, in many ways, contradicted my experience as an artist up to that point; I had to create my work in buses, in forests, in subway stations, changing the places where I worked almost every day. It was then that I discovered the importance of the body. In nomadic circumstances the body is the important factor, but eventually not only that: what is important is the need (desire, one might describe it) to maintain the capacity to work and think creatively. One could define that as a body-centric process of art making. After a nomadic experience the body becomes once again the center of that which one is.

The incidents that I described were *The Fear of Artistic Practice, The Non-reality of Danger, The Trace of Danger, Changing Identities, The Imminent Danger, The Presence of Death*. All these have created a new frame of reference of how to perceive reality. The way I perceived Danger, Identity, and Death was never the same again.

The most crucial conclusion of the above is the relationship between Danger and Identity. What one is facing in nomadism is the way others perceive you: being a nomad means that you are constantly profiled and simultaneously you are profiling the other. The process of identifying the Other is a source of danger; a wrong judgment, a miscalculation could be fatal. Walking in the mountain and meeting other people or animals creates an embarrassment and an instant need to recognize the other: these awkward and tense moments of trying to create an identity for the person you meet is crucial to one's survival. The same is true early in the morning near Omonia Square in the center of Athens or at the border between Greece and Albania. Who is the Other approaching you, what are his/her demands, should you feel threatened? If you miss something in recognizing this identity, then danger could be imminent.

After all, contemporary nomadism is nothing but a quest for identity. Identity is discovered (if it ever does get discovered) with risks and dangers. These dangers are the outcome of the effort to survive in an always-changing living environment.

NOTES:

1. Ulrich Beck, *World Risk Society* (Cambridge, UK: Polity Press), 1999.
2. Giorgios Alexias, *The Sociology of the Body* (Athens: Pedio), 2011.
3. I refer to the way Turner perceives bodiment as a form of experientiality of the body (236, 1995). Bodiment is the way the body becomes a component of social involvement and at the same time a society in itself.
4. *Visual March to Prespes* is a nomadic art-process that is been realized since 2007 in the area of Prespes. The activity organizes annually in Prespes visual activities that explore the landscape, culture, and ecological dimension of the area. Every year a series of events culminate in the weekly process in the area of Prespes where artists, students, hike in the area, exploring it as a landscape shaped by its contrasting reality. At the same time *Visual March to Prespes* establishes a network of exchange between the instructors and the students of the Department of Visual and Applied Arts (University of Western Macedonia), the local community, as well as the broader Greek, Balkan, and international community.
5. The notion of the collector of incidents was introduced by the Russian film director Andrei Tarkovsky in his film *Sacrifice* (1986). The collector of incidents is a nomad who interprets his/her status of transition as an opportunity to broaden his/her spiritual background by gathering objects and experiences as a process of self-definition.

Yannis Ziogas is a painter and assistant professor in the Department of Visual and Applied Arts at the University of Western Macedonia. He is the author of *Byzantine Malevich*, *Tarkovsky in Chalkis,* and *The Diary of a ΠΔ 407/80*. His work has been exhibited in Greece, the U.S., and many European countries.

Mekbib Gemeda

Crossing cultures: reflections on language

As a traveler crossing languages and cultures, I have often reflected on the cultural elements that shape my identity and inform my perception and expression. Language in particular has been a central feature of my transformational experience. Language is the frame of reference at the core of culture that communicates beliefs and values and determines the behavior of a group. Acquiring language brings one closer to understanding and adopting culture. Gore Vidal's character in his novel, *Creation*, describes it well: "Fortunately, Caraka knew enough Aryan words to help me begin to comprehend not only a new language but a new world, for it is the language of a people that tells us most about what gods they worship and what sort of men they are or would like to be." My experience learning different languages has been a process not only of learning about different cultures and cultural experiences but also of forming different identities and a sense of connection and disconnection.

Mother Tongue and Early Identity

Amharic is my mother tongue. Although it was not the only language spoken in the household while I was growing up, Amharic was the primary language. As it was a household of mixed heritage, I grew up listening to the Oromo language as well. The Amharic of Addis Ababa had its own flavor, distinguishing itself from provincial Amharic as a more sophisticated urban multicultural language. Italian was another presence in the household. My father worked with Italians for most of his life; he was involved in the construction business and had many Italian friends. Our family was close to an Italian family who lived next door. They would spend almost every other evening at our house deep into the evening talking, drinking coffee, and smoking cigarettes. They were born in Ethiopia after the war and spoke Amharic. So the conversations flowed across Italian and Amharic depending on the topic. Things the adults did not want us kids to hear were spoken in Italian.

Some Italian words and phrases remained with me and found their way into my Croatian and English until they disappeared all together over time. When I moved to Rome from Yugoslavia, I found the Italian language easy to learn, I think, because of this early exposure to the language that was somehow kept hidden yet accessible when needed.

English was taught in primary school parallel to Amharic. We learned the English and Amharic alphabets at the same time and continued with English lessons throughout school. Depending on the level of rigor of the school, students were able to acquire substantive knowledge of English by middle school. In high school and college, English was the primary language in which all subjects were taught. Amharic took a secondary place. Amharic grammar and literature was taught as a unit.

English also became the language of descent, rebellion against cultural norms, expression of the desire for western culture, for freedom. We would speak it interlaced with Amharic. We found expressions in it that we did not seem to find in Amharic. Acquiring English opened for us global dimensions, a sense that we had identities beyond the national. It did distance us, however, at the same time, from our local cultural mooring, limiting our exploration of the local cultural dictionary and moving us further away from provincial and national expressions.

Yugoslavia

Through hard work, some cunning, and a lot of luck I managed to secure a scholarship in the early 1980s to study film in Yugoslavia and slip away from the grip of the brutal dictatorship in Ethiopia. Yugoslavia was supposed to be a brief stop on the way to freedom. I could not imagine at the moment the extent to which my experience in Yugoslavia would define me. The experience of being alone, engulfed in a completely different culture and language, was an overwhelming and paralyzing experience. As I walked across Zrinjevac Park on my second day in Zagreb, unprepared for that snowy Sunday in my skimpy shoes and clothes, my new gray Austro-Hungarian reality slowly sank in. The snow, the tram, the sounds of Slavic language surrounding me were all completely new and overpowering. These experiences outside of our cultural bubble, while deeply disconcerting, provide us with a unique opportunity to learn not only about other cultures, but our own.

Learning the Croatian language did not come easily. I found the learning better done through intensive socializing and a more focused approach to learning the language. I decided not to rely on the simplistic scripted language lessons that were also designed to introduce us to the culture of the place. I forced myself to speak Croatian exclusively and engaged in an extensive effort to learn the literary and visual culture. I had a choice to socialize with a good number of Ethiopian students in Zagreb at the time. But they were huddled together for safety and comfort. Leaving Ethiopia at a time of extreme repression and persecution, I did not find comfort in the language and culture. I longed for exploring other realities and cultures and threw myself wholly to this effort.

It is evident that global diffusion of western culture codified through music, film, and a common world view has brought together into a shared cultural plane generations that grew up from the 60s onward. Like many of the young people I was to meet in my travels, I grew up inspired by the

American and English music scene and American films mesmerized me and allowed me to share a new global cultural reality. I socialized with my friends and colleagues during these college years in Croatia around this shared cultural campfire.

The notion of transformational experience brings with it the question of cultural identity. Having engaged extensively in cultural activities reading and writing, and working as a producer in radio and films, I acquired more than a superficial understanding of the culture in Croatia and the former Yugoslavia. My cultural identity was transformed in the process. With the acquisition of a new language, I had adopted a new culture, an appreciation of its contextual dimensions and the capacity to think and dream in it. I left it with the heavy heart of one deserting his own, leaving behind the familiar for the uncertain. But it seems I carried this world with me, I did not cease to think and dream in it and to struggle with the question of cultural identity.

English

Although English was part of my early primary education and the language of my cultural adolescence, total immersion into the language and culture upon immigrating to the U.S. presented me another opportunity for exploring my cultural identity. English became my professional medium as I pursued graduate education and commenced my professional life. American English in particular exposed me to the culture of direct, low context communication and efficiency. Coming from high context cultures, I was shocked to hear the phrase "good for you" so sincerely mouthed. In Ethiopia this phrase would imply insincerity in sharing someone's good fortune. On the other hand, I appreciated the direct, efficient flight-control approach to communication. There are no Ethiopian or Croatian equivalents of Strunk and White. I often complain about the lack of efficiency in Croatian or Amharic newspapers whose sentences stretch to paragraphs with the message unfolding in the final words. I was reminded, however, that this was not the only feature of English. It is an evolving language constantly changing by adoption. It was the language that attracted me and gave me a glimpse of the multicultural America of William Saroyan, Vladimir Nabokov, Raymond Carver, and Ralph Ellison long before I came to the United States, and that continues to evolve with the work of authors like Ha Jin.

Now that I have settled in the U.S. and call it my home, the English language permeates all facets of my life. It is the language of my children and therefore the language of parental love and affection, the language of friendship nurturing many friendships that I have cultivated over the years, some with Americans who speak the language with a foreign accent like myself. It has replaced in large part the Croatian that I shared with my wife in the domesticity of everyday life.

The languages I learned across my cultural formation shaped the separate identities through which I perceive reality and form my expressions. My childhood memories and dreams are locked in the Amharic of my childhood. Amharic is the language of this longing for lost childhood and innocence, longing for parents and family, and for perpetually unreachable expressions in the mother tongue. Deep sorrow and pain still find their expression for me in the sounds of this language. Croatian is the language of my youth, of love found and lost, of adventure and nostalgia for youth and for connection. English became my destination, the land after the long journey at sea, the language for recapping the experience. As I reflected on this project, it was English that revealed itself to mediate the process.

Cultural transformation is not merely the presence of multiple identities. It involves the creation of new identities that synthesize cultural experiences. While the experience of migrating and negotiating multiple identities could be schizophrenic at times, the transcendental understanding of the shared human condition that flows through cultures makes it a worthwhile endeavor. I feel that I have acquired, through my exposure to multiple language and cultural experiences, the global identity that I was longing for as a youth. The exposure gives me the constant urge and the plasticity to connect with people from different cultures and walks of like. Yet, in the end, I feel simultaneously disconnected, not belonging to one place in particular, perpetually longing.

Mekbib Gemeda is a social critic and activist who has focused his professional life on exploring social inequities particularly in health care. Mekbib grew up in Addis Ababa, Ethiopia. He studied theatre and film in Ethiopia and Yugoslavia and did his graduate work in the U.S. in communication and culture. He has lived and worked in the New York City area for the past 22 years. He currently holds an appointment at Eastern Virginia Medical School in Norfolk, VA, where he continues his work on health equity. As an author and filmmaker he has worked on a number of fiction and short documentary films. He has also worked as a radio producer in Croatia.

Mahita El Bacha Urieta

Rooted in Disorientation

The following text was written intermittently, over a period of several months, while at 'home,' at various different offices and hotels, on different buses and trains, at different airports and on different airplanes in Abu Dhabi (U.A.E.); Beirut (Lebanon); Frankfurt, Dusseldorf, and Cologne (Germany); Amsterdam (Netherlands); in Singapore, Phnom Penh, and Siem Reap (Cambodia); and Hue and Hoi An (Vietnam).

"A good traveler has no fixed plans and is not intent on arriving."[1]

Growing Up A Compulsive Nomad

I was born in Beirut, Lebanon, the year in which the war started, into a family of artists, to a Spanish mother and a Lebanese father. I guess that my cultural make up, which is informed by two different continents, two countries, two cultures, and two languages, predisposed me to have personal connections to two different 'homes.' I was the youngest of three girls. The war brought with it unpredictability, insecurity, fear, and panic among society, my family included. Our daily lives were transformed by the lack of basic needs such as electricity and water and food, as well as hospital beds and health care supplies. With this also came diseases and I became quite ill at only a few months of age.

At the time, my parents were engaged in charitable work and peaceful activism in Beirut while also working hard and looking after our young family. My two sisters were at boarding school in the hills outside Beirut and caring for me adequately in Beirut became increasingly difficult in the absence of the basic means of survival. Hospitals were full of victims of war and were controlled by militiamen from all sorts of different political parties. Weapons abounded within hospitals as all these political parties forced their injured family members and friends for treatment upon medics, often causing confrontation and actual shootings within hospitals.

Beirut was unsafe.

In this climate, my parents decided that the best solution for me would be to fly me to my mother's family in the Pyrenees to live with my aunt in Northern Spain where I could be properly looked after.

This journey was my first... I was only a few months old.

I ended up living in Spain for several years, learning to speak Spanish and going to school there and considering Spain to be my home country. My father, mother, and sisters visited me when possible and one day, four years later, they picked me up to return to live in Lebanon with them.

This was the second time that I was leaving 'home' to go and live somewhere else... which I was being told was 'home.'

I still remember refusing to set foot on the ground upon arrival in Beirut and feeling totally out of place, fearing my surroundings and all the new sights, sounds, and smells that now made up the fabric of my new life. I never quite adapted to life in Beirut...

The following years were packed with regular travel, changes of 'home,' of country, of school, of scenery, of socio-cultural context.

Over the years, I have lived in Lebanon, Spain, Cyprus, Tunisia, U.K., and the U.A.E.

In common sense language, identification is constructed on the back of a recognition of some common origin or shared characteristics with another person or group, or with an ideal, and with the natural closure of solidarity and allegiance established on this foundation. In contrast with the 'naturalism' of this definition, the discursive approach sees identification as a construction, a process never completed—always 'in process.' It is not determined in the sense that it can always be 'won' or 'lost,' sustained or abandoned. Though not without its determinate conditions of existence, including the material and symbolic resources required to sustain it, identification is conditional, lodged in contingency. Once secured, it does not obliterate difference.[2]

What's your name? What does it mean?
Where are you from? Where do you call home?

My name is Mahita. It means a small Maha. Maha is a poetic Arabic term that describes a woman's beautiful eyes, referring to the beautiful eyes of the wild gazelle of the desert called *maha*. 'Ita' is a Spanish feminine diminutive.

Every time I meet someone, wherever this might be in the world, I am asked exactly the same questions, almost always in exactly the same order: "What's your name? What does it mean? Where are you from? Where do you call home?" I always answer by first explaining my name, and second, saying that my father is from Lebanon and my mother is from Spain. The following question always is: "Where do you call home?" I first used to enter into long explanations, but over recent years, having become bored hearing myself give the same answers, I started to answer that I don't call anywhere home and that I am not sure what the notion of home actually means or constitutes: "for me, home is wherever I might be standing at any given moment, generally inside my own shoes: My home is standing in my own shoes."

As I was growing up, I found myself resisting any kind of labeling and classification by others as they encountered me and tried to figure out my identity. I actively refused to give simple answers and always kept people guessing. It was indeed a form of resistance—first unconscious—to being limited and put into a category that might bind me, lock me up, limit me and take away my dynamic and free-flowing exercise in identity formation. It was a form of rebellion, especially in a place like Lebanon, where conflict has always been fueled by notions of local identification, sectarianism, and 'being part of this place and that religion as opposed to all the others.' I have always wanted to remain 'neither one thing nor the other' and not the combination of both, either. Just 'nothing in particular' and what I chose to be is my own prerogative and could change with the seasons.

My identity is my business… it is my sport… it is my project…

With time, I have come to believe that our need for a 'home' might just be culturally induced and acquired.

Do we, humans, truly need a home or do we just feel, think, and live as our environment and culture teach us to? Having never had a sense of belonging in my life, I noticed that with time I started to feel pressured to address this matter and to actually find myself a home or create one for myself, but for this I had to first choose a spot on earth in which to root myself and that was—and still is—no small challenge for me.

Then came a strong feeling of disorientation: I would be drawn to one place—sometimes London, other times the South of Spain, or even the Southern Islands of Thailand, and would then feel ejected away to another place.

I finally realized that I was forcing myself into choosing a place in order to somehow 'belong' to it, but that effectively this did not come naturally to me and that I should stop tormenting myself and let go of this pressure and just be as I only know how to be.

Confused, lost, schizophrenic, uprooted I may be, or just free, flexible, multi-cultural, always in flux, always searching, or just accepting the fact that I am what I am and how I am and feeling at peace with this fact.

Eventually, I have also come to realize that if we have an innate need for a home or at least for a sense of home, the most reliable home might be within ourselves; a sort of spiritual, internal feeling, a rootedness to our essential intangible bond to life and bond to the metaphysical dimension that also makes us up—us humans—and that actually constitutes our free, unbound, and timeless dimension.

I am very aware of the limited reliability of earthly 'homes,' of the ephemeral nature of our lives and of our materiality. Everything changes and everything passes; everything fades and everything ends. I (We), am also changing, moving, passing, and soon 'ending' and it is paradoxical and almost impossible to bind myself to any place, to any one core because of my nature. The other dimension within me, the boundless, limitless, open, and free dimension within me (and within every human being) seems like a more suitable home for my nature and certainly seems more deeply reflective of who I (We) am at a deeper level: connected to earth but not bound by it or to it.

I am aware of the fact that psychologically, my keenness on up-rootedness has, in addition to being a form of resistance to being 'stuck' anywhere, quite probably served me as a form of constant escapism. It has served as a mechanism to keep me 'out' of action in environments that did not feel comfortable to me. It has protected me from having to connect with contexts that I did not want to be part of over the years. Just as mobility has become a way of life, escapism and living in my own cocoon have also become a way of life for me. Luckily I have embraced them today through my being fully aware of them and of how they came into being and how they actually served me all those years.

> [Identification] accepts that identities are never unified and, in late modern times, increasingly fragmented and fractured; never singular but multiply constructed across different, often intersecting and antagonistic, discourses, practices, and positions.[3]

Looking at the world today, within the climate of globalization (which started centuries ago but which has sped up in a major way over the past decade or so) and what some call the opening up of the world onto itself thanks to information technology, mass migration, and all the other symptoms and mechanisms of globalization, there are also communities closing in on themselves and cultural struggles taking place where communities want to separate into their own, single, 'pure' community and culture and live under their own banners.

There are also currents of extreme religious identifications in many parts of the world, fueling fanatical movements of independence and self-determination under banners of 'pure,' cultural orthodoxy, often also choosing a territory in which to root these 'pure' communities and fighting for the control of this territory, this culture, and this community. I see all those tendencies as limiting traps and as only fueling ignorance, isolationism, violence, and hatred.

In fact, this context makes me feel privileged to not be bound to or by any culture, territory, or religion, to not have a rigid, fixed sense of self and to, instead, be able to stay free of such limitations, able to constantly change and grow, to stay open to life and to all its generous diversity, to live with a constant sense of wonder and open ended-ness where the search always continues and possibilities remain endless…

Indeed it is very challenging at times to exist in such a way, but I seem to prefer difficulty to a finite, locked-up, and fully resolved existence.

Mobility, Up-rootedness and Otherness
Transnationalism and *Dépaysement*[4]

The best way for me to describe the migrating, multi-referential, and dynamic quality of my identity is as a 'transnational identity,' which is constantly expanding and adding new socio-cultural and geographical reference points to an already multifarious root. I have always created and continue to make connections that cross geographical, cultural, and political borders. I maintain multiple familial, economic, social, organizational, ideological, and political relations that span borders. This is the most essential quality of my life.

At first I was too young to choose mobility and travel, as the first travels I undertook were initiated by my parents and were in search of security. I would be packed-up and sent to a new country, enrolled into a new school among new 'friends,' in a totally new socio-cultural context, and what I did was instinctively adapt. I adapted to every context without question, never really thinking about the difficulties and the challenges that each change brought me. There was no time for that. I had to adapt and survive. I just fit in in whatever way I had to fit in, each time.

Later in life I found myself, first unconsciously, seeking movement and change, constantly needing to abruptly interrupt the current of my life and to generate a total upheaval, which often brought with it movement, travel, relocation, and another 'starting over' for me.

Having been accustomed to constantly breaking out from a young age, moving on, and starting over, I probably never learned to stay in one place, to be rooted in a given location, to be grounded in a community and in a particular context. I gradually became the eternal 'nomad' which I now am and found myself, when unable to move countries, actually moving home, within the same city, sometimes as often as twice a year.

Do I Travel to Work
or
Do I Work to Travel?
Nothing happens coincidentally. In retrospect, I find it remarkable that I ended up working in the international arts sector, among a community of

fellow, eternal travelers and working within programs and formats that were often defined by their ephemeral or traveling nature, often also having an inter-cultural quality in addition to their international scope.

In the late 1980s, amid the violence in Lebanon, I moved to Tunisia and then Beirut. During this time I started to become more aware of the distinct quality of my life which was that of "not quite belonging," not fitting-in, not feeling part of any place, any group, or any community. It was a difficult time for me as I was a teenager who seemed to need to feel less like an 'outsider' but did not know how to.

I was hoping for a major 'escape' abroad to carry out my university studies after finally completing my school years, but my parents insisted that I spend the next three years in Lebanon, as the long Lebanese war was declared finished.

I studied history and archaeology of the Eastern Mediterranean at the American University of Beirut. I worked on introducing pan-Arabic artists to the art market in Beirut, then worked on the production and management of 'non-European'—as they were being called in Europe at the time—culturally specific, multi-art form festivals throughout the United Kingdom.

This work introduced me to the policies of cultural diversity and access, equal opportunities, and the related jargon and programs, which were very much of the moment in Europe at that time. This is when I realized how— in spite of their 'supposed' good intentions and the fact that they were meant to change the 'exclusive' status quo within arts and culture—these policies and their linguistics and related programs were only perpetuating exclusion and only enabling tokenistic action here and there and maintaining differences and cultural and social segregation within the cultural and arts sectors and ultimately within wider society in the U.K. and also in wider Europe.

This subject fascinated me and I decided to undertake an M.A. in Arts Policy and Management and to focus on the Cultural Diversity policy of the Arts Council England which I analytically critiqued, departing from the language and jargon that this policy generated and applied on the arts and culture sectors of the U.K., which in turn transmitted a discriminatory set of values through a series of programs and projects that were, ironically, initially aimed at stopping discrimination.

I subsequently worked with organizations that changed the mono-cultural nature of the arts and culture sector in London which, actually, has a very culturally mixed population, and that focused on revisiting the art history and archives of the U.K. and to complete them by introducing to them the contributions of immigrant artists from different cultural descents who had been previously excluded from that history and who had often not even been recognized at all in the U.K. The other aspect of some of the organization's work was to support young contemporary artists from so called 'ethnic minorities'—as they tended to be called at that time in the U.K.—who had difficulties in being exhibited and recognized locally.

Following this work, I decided to leave the U.K. and was, around the same time, introduced to the director of a contemporary art biennial in the U.A.E. who offered me a job in her hometown in order to coordinate the Biennale which was to be international in scope with a strong Arabic element... I have since done a multitude of other jobs, many of them in Arab countries.

Today, my career seems to still be defined and shaped by travel. Or, did I choose this type of career and the multiple episodes that constitute it because it helped 'normalize' my constant need for travel and my dependence on up-rootedness?

At one point, during my many travels, I realized that I lived a life where it was so easy not to go deeper into matters at hand, not to focus on anything for too long as 'going away' was always just around the corner and leaving was a constant theme. I seemed to always choose short-term jobs because leaving was in fact always easier for me than staying.

Ironically, over recent years, I ended up basing myself in Abu Dhabi, in a place where—at least for non-nationals—life is not about being rooted, it is about being here just for professional reasons, about a temporary life, short-term planning and an eventual, ever-looming departure. It is ironic that in my attempt to stay in one place for more than a year or two, I seem to have chosen a place which, in itself, does not offer any sense of rootedness, permanence, or home.

When I first came to the U.A.E., I knew so little about the country but seem to have been captivated by the total *dépaysement* which it provided, not least because of its unique cultural and social paradoxes which I find very interesting, but also because of the conditions of residing here as an expatriate (which is how non-U.A.E. Nationals are called here): one has the official status of an 'outsider' and is here only temporarily.

Many aspects of the politics, society, and culture of this place are very challenging to me as they conflict with my views and my ideals. However, these challenges, paired with the total *dépaysement* and ephemeral nature of my situation seem to have responded to my interest in 'cultural intrigue' and my need for disconnection and open-endedness.

I am a traveling nomad and always will be and I do not have or want roots anywhere in the world. I seem to have accepted this today.

This sense of *dépaysement*, which I considered to be a particular quality of my personal experience, seems to be more common and maybe even a 'global tendency' today, toward increased mobility, disorientation, and gradual loss of a distinct sense of place around the world.

Globalization of Arts and Culture

"In societies where modern conditions of production prevail, all of life presents itself as an immense accumulation of spectacles. Everything that was directly lived has moved away into a representation."[5]

On one hand there seems to be increasing mobility by an increased number of people who travel for work (some of them don't really have a choice), or travel for leisure because more of us can afford to do so nowadays. On the other hand, it seems that although we might travel more, everywhere is actually gradually starting to look and feel quite similar. Our world is increasingly shaped by globalization and the standardization of everything.

In the arts, perhaps, the most useful format and platform for the presentation of art to illustrate the ever more globalized arts and culture sectors is the 'international art biennial.' Other formats that are also tightly linked to travel and to globalization are the multitude of new 'artist residency' programs as well as the 'international art fairs,' and the trend of art galleries and auction-houses, mainly from the U.S.A. and Europe, opening in secondary locations in Asia, Arab countries, and others.

From my experiences, different art biennials impact different aspects of society, the local art world, local artists, the international art world, etc., depending on where those biennials are staged, who is behind them, how they are financed and promoted by, what their real objective might be, how old or young they are, and what their curatorial mechanism are.

We cannot speak of the Venice Biennale on the same footing as we might speak of the Sharjah Biennial or the Thessaloniki Biennale for example.

One thing is sure: travel and mobility are imperative for and are part and parcel of the concept and format of biennials. They define, condition, and are central to the nature of the format and experience of biennials and at times also their aesthetic. However, a 'bubble' is created by biennials all over the world, which heavily shapes and conditions the particular travel experience engendered by one biennial or the other. When an 'arts person' takes off to a biennial, an art fair, or the launch of a new art gallery abroad (this can also be said of music festivals and happenings in the performing arts world), he/she exists within a sort of curated travel bubble which is composed of associations, projections, and arts related concerns and notions which separate that person from the actual place where he/she might be heading toward and from the journey there.

This is the paradoxical implied promise of biennials. Yes they represent international art practice but they also take place in a specific local context and this is often their only differentiating quality setting them apart from one another.

Biennials are generally intended to provide a new look at the local context and a different perspective, but what ends up happening is that they create a tribe that continuously travels, is never long enough in any location to connect with it or actually properly 'land' in it in any meaningful manner, is too distracted by thinking about the next international stop-over, and the multiple projects that they might be working on in several other locations.

What good comes of biennials then and how reasonable is it today to invest so much in their development and production while money is lacking in more fundamental areas of the arts and culture sectors?

There are, however, compelling aspects to what biennials have generated. It is really fascinating to see work from so many different parts of the world, sometimes dealing with one particular theme through totally different media and production processes, different aesthetics, and different points of view. There is a whole generation of artists that one can almost call 'biennial artists' as they are so often shown at biennials around the world. There are also curators who are very much involved in biennials and creative industry companies that one also comes across over and over again taking part in the production of the promotion of biennials. And of course the independent and institutional gatekeepers you find in Turkey, Lebanon, Dubai, Lagos, São Paulo, Barcelona, Delhi, and many others and who are connected to the network of the 'biennial crowd,' the 'biennial industry,' and who all collaborate with one another time and time again.

They have all contributed to the formulation of a discourse around the curation and critique of the 'international,' 'global' contemporary art practice that is shown at biennials everywhere and have all helped to link up practitioners from across countries and boundaries on all the various biennial platforms.

Only after some years, it might be time for this rich and varied echo-system to try to push beyond what is becoming a repetitive ritual and a certain *déjà-vu* with every new biennial edition that is inaugurated.

Biennials might have reached a somewhat stagnant stage where it might be worth it for us all to look outside this bubble and envisage the next step forward. How do we build on what biennials have achieved? What might be a more progressive and more engaged and engaging way of moving forward innovatively? How can we push this conversation to the next level?

What day is it? Where am I?

When one travels a lot and often, this affects their energy levels, ability to ground themselves, their attention span, their ability to focus, to sleep, to be productive and creative, to connect, and to relate.

After years of making an effort to actually attend openings, launches, inaugurations, and the likes, I now religiously try to avoid them and visit only some exhibitions, biennials, art fairs, etc., at my own pace and stay in contact only with individuals from the 'art world' with whom I truly have a connection that is solid enough for us to not have to depend on occasional, fleeting displays of connection, attention, and affection in the midst of arts events.

A World Without Boundaries

I was particularly struck by one of the questions that was put forward by apexart for this publication: *In considering the creative world and the business world, what is the actual possibility of a truly multicultural society and a world without boundaries?*

As I travel and during my current travels in particular, as I was thinking about some of the questions raised by apexart and the answers that were being triggered in me, it was confirmed again that we are already and actually a truly multicultural world, a species without boundaries.

However, sadly, our organized societies are not without racial, ethnic, cultural, social, economics, and other divides.

The problem seems to lie in our minds and in the way in which our minds function, perhaps only for the sake of survival: human beings conceive of systems that seem to be designed, constructed, and established mostly in the service of certain select groups above others—systems that are informed by notions of cultural-centrism and racial and or social superiority, all of which contribute to institutionalizing difference and inequality at local and global levels.

Still, when one encounters another on the other side of the globe, the human connection is ignited and it is strong. It is capable of achieving a great deal through communication, compassion, cooperation, and collaboration.

If only this strongest of bonds could be given its chance on a micro and macro level for a peaceful, all encompassing union of equal human beings across lands, continents, oceans, deserts, and mountains; across cultures, societies, genders, and age groups… We might then be able to truly experience and be an active part of what I think apexart was referring to by "a truly multicultural society and a world without boundaries."

The question that arises for me here is: as human beings, are we actually conditioned to differentiate, separate, compete, and defend in order to survive?

I don't believe that as humans we are able to surpass our nature and the potentials that we were born with. I believe that the potential for everything that we conceive, manifest, and realize was meant this way, including our destructive and violent tendencies. I don't mean to justify destruction or violence here or to imply that everything is programmed to be as it is and that all that is meant to be will be.

I do think that we have a part to play. We are indeed agents in our own lives… I am only trying to understand: why is it that consistently, through history, since the dawn of time, men and women have organized themselves in different groups and set themselves apart from each other, defining themselves through different sets of beliefs, cultural determinants, and socio-cultural qualities, fighting each other for hundreds of years and until today?

Isn't it just our human survival instinct that imposes on us this way of being? Do we even have it in our DNA to realize the ideal of a boundless multicultural world?

Another question that arises is about the acquired sense of belonging to a place that seems to assume that at some level 'places' are cohesive, homogeneous, and 'pure' and that their borders actually delineate them, keeping them 'protected' and differentiated from 'other' territories.

(I only mention Vietnam and Singapore in the following section because I was recently there. Many other countries could also illustrate the points that I attempted to make here.)

In my most recent travels, to places such as Singapore and Vietnam (in very different ways as these places are so utterly different from one another),

I was starkly reminded of the many internal and often intangible layers that actually consitute places and identities. For example the perceived 'local' attributes, those that are identified as 'national' attributes and those that are conscious constructs, for example: the packaged tourist experiences, the cultural archetypes, and typical local cultural experiences that are exhibited and sold to tourists in Vietnam (or those being formulated as 'local identity' in the U.A.E.).

Another example is the Singaporean 'sense of place' that has been developed by the government of Singapore in order to attract foreign business and investment and expatriate immigrants in order to help make Singapore the place for easy business, a haven for 'high quality standards' and high quality of life, a 'cosmopolitan' place made up of a cultural melting pot, etc.

Beneath this surface are very different realities, as in every place in the world. Places, localities, 'countries' are much more multi-layered than we might think. Singapore is not what is seems to be, neither is Vietnam. They, like all other places on this planet, commodify certain aspects of their culture, of their 'image' and these become more accessible to outsiders than the more complex and deeper realities of the place. (And some commodify selected aspects of their culture or project new qualities onto their culture and sell it to their own people.) So much was projected onto Vietnam in relation to the 'Vietnam War,' making this aspect of the country's past one of its themes and making trauma and pain a commodity to package and sell to outsiders. To a certain extent, some of this is also true of Lebabnon, and Beirut in particular.

Singapore sells the idea of opportunity, prosperity, and luxury to outsiders but beneath the surface, and for local citizens, it is a totally different story. The society seems to be organized under ethnic groupings and there is a great deal of exclusion within the socio-economic and political systems, which are dominated by the local Chinese community. Multiculturalism is not celebrated in Singapore as one might think. What seems to be celebrated is a heavily capitalist lifestyle and an American-style consumer culture. The modern metropolis is slowly but surely closing in on beautiful old neighborhoods, and radically changing the face of Singapore into the 'global,' 'non-place' that looks like so many other fast 'developing' locations of our 21st century world.

We have to look beyond what countries project of themselves so that we can excavate the multifaceted nature of place and of borders including the somewhat intangible but very real ones. We also have to try to look beyond our assumptions and projections. But is this humanly possible? Can we perceive and can we 'know' or attempt to know without, at least at first, projecting?

If we wanted to look at travel, movement, place, borders, multiculturalism, and identity, we might want to delve into the nature and quality of all the layers that actually constitute cultures, territories, and often also borders.

We make assumptions about 'places' and about what defines them and makes them up as locations and as cultural entities but we should not fool ourselves with the idea that our worldly territory is a clearly cut mosaic of places separated by clear linear borders and that our identities are associated with one or with another place and that when we travel we travel from point A to point B.

There is so much more movement taking place and in so many directions even as one moves within a small territory, or from point A to point B, not least the 'movement' and other processes that occur internally in the mind of the traveler, making sense of change as he or she moves, being 'modified' and modifying his and her surroundings as he or she encounters it.

We are complex beings and our environment and its intrinsic constructs are even more complicated... let alone all our projections on places and on people as we travel within them, across them and through their loaded layers.

NOTES:

1. Lao Tazu: According to Chinese tradition, Lao Tzu lived in the 6th century BCE. Historians variously contend that Lao Tzu is a synthesis of multiple historical figures, that he is a mythical figure, or that he actually lived in the 5th-4th century BCE, concurrent with the Hundred Schools of Thought and Warring States Period.
2. Stuart Hall, "Who needs an 'Identity'," in *Questions of Cultural Identity*, ed. Stuart Hall and Paul du Gay (London: Sage, 1996), 1-17.
3. Ibid.
4. *Dépaysement*: French word that has no translation to the English language and means the feeling that comes from not being in one's home country, the feeling of being a foreigner, the disorientation that comes from a total change of scenery, the feeling of being in exile, of being exiled.
5. Guy Debord, "Separation Perfected," chapter 1 in *La Société du Spectacle* (Paris: Éditions Buchet-Chastel, 1967).

Mahita El Bacha Urieta is curator and cultural design, policy, and management specialist and founding director of ONDA Culture Consultancy. With an academic background in archaeology and arts and culture policy, she has worked in music, arts education, the visual arts, and cross-cultural initiatives mainly in Europe and the Middle East. Current projects include institutional and cultural program design for the Beit Beirut city museum and war memorial in Lebanon and the Central Park development in Abu Dhabi. Previously Arts Strategist at the Abu Dhabi Authority for Culture Heritage and curator of the Thessaloniki Biennale in Greece, 2011. She developed a cultural policy for the U.A.E., consulted for the British Council International and coordinated the Sharjah Biennial of Contemporary Art, U.A.E. (2004-07). She was winner of the Abraaj Capital Art Prize in 2010 and curator of *Arabise Me*, arts festival, V&A Museum, London (2006), and Bluecoat Art Centre, Liverpool, UK (2008); Manager of Manifesta 6, European Biennial, Nicosia, Cyprus (2005-06) and several exhibitions with the Institute of International Visual Art (inIVA) in London, including *Fault Lines: Contemporary African Art and Shifting Landscapes*, 50th Venice Biennale (2003).

Sebastien Sanz de Santamaria

Global Nomad Lady

It was at the International School of Amsterdam, as a teenager, that I first heard the term *global nomad*. Having been raised by parents working in the foreign service, I had a childhood jumping from one country to another and attended schools with kids like myself, from other countries with families working in diplomatic or military corps, and international business. My school friends were coming from one place (or many places, prior) and eventually going to another place henceforth.

One day, we middle school students were sent to the auditorium to listen to an invited speaker tell us that we were all *global nomads*. From what I remember, she was a psycho-social researcher invited by our school's administration to talk to us about this particular demographic. When she mentioned this newly coined term, she would do so in a wide-eyed and excited manner, as if she was conducting a magic show, turning a bouquet of flowers into a white dove that immediately flew off the stage. During her presentation, she proceeded to explain the social advantages and disadvantages of living such a lifestyle. I assume she pointed out the benefits of having multilingual capabilities, quick adaptability to environments, and the privilege of being exposed to a myriad of different cultures and societies, but I don't remember any of those points. What stuck with me was the dark side of this way of living, a series of saddening statistics of high divorce rates, difficulty settling down, job changes, insecurity, kids (we kids) having difficulty at school, even descriptions on the inability to make decisions. What also marked me was her equal enthusiasm in delivering such bad news. Like a doctor giving a patient the diagnosis of a terminal disease with a big smile and a healthy pat on the back. Basically, global nomads had some form of genetic malfunction of refusing to ever settle down. Like some curse, doomed to roam the lands and live difficult, complicated lives.

Reflecting on this event of my youth, despite its darker aspects, I can safely state that it helped me to define the world I had been living in for the entirety of my childhood. It would guide me towards explaining to others where I was from; or more importantly where I had been. This was a difference that I was not aware of back then. When someone would ask me "Where are you from?" I would always take a moment to answer (I still do, but it's only for show). This delay came from the notion that where one is born and where one is raised are generically considered to be the same place, and I had to mentally recalculate my differences each and every time I was asked this question.

Jumping to the present day and looking back, much as I shuddered to global nomad lady's statements on our inevitably destabilized lives, I've come to terms with the fact that she was pretty much on point. I settled in New York City more than a decade ago, and despite it being the longest time I have spent in one city, I have never seemed to really settle down. I've averaged moving apartments every two years, sometimes by choice, other times not. I just moved again a month ago, damn it! I'm like a 150-pound chrome-steel ball in a giant pinball game that is this metropolis. In addition to this perpetual jumping bean lifestyle, I co-founded an artist residency program three years ago, aimed at supporting both local and visiting international artists through a de-centralized multi-layered format, bringing people, resources, and networks that span the five boroughs to the fingertips of our artists. As such, I've inherently created a system that puts artists through the same type of nomadic environment

I've been living in since day one and have done so in a city that pretty much mirrors the entire planet in 789 square kilometers. Two decades later, I have created my own little international school for artists in my own mini version of the world. I now understand global nomad lady and her enthused vision of who we were to be as individuals.

That I have fulfilled the prophecy with respect to me being a lost soul in this vast and diverse land, one could say that I do qualify in a variety of her statistics. But it's important to note that it has also positively facilitated my participation in a creative industry that is extremely busy with cross-cultural interaction. Within the field of "residency" (a relatively young concept), nomadic and ever-moving initiatives are crucial to its existence. Residencies were initially engineered as a means of escape for artists, providing a haven from the distractions of daily life in order to concentrate on the creation of work. Nowadays, there are a variety of different formats, each serving different purposes. The individuals participating in these environments are all sensitive to the factors and conditions that this itinerant world incurs; it would not function otherwise. As such, the creative industry snuggles up to nomad-ism because nomad-ism nurtures and feeds into creativity, more than other ways of living.

This phenomenon can be exemplified with a simple observation on memory. When traveling to an unknown place, awareness is heightened as ones person shifts into ultra-sensitive mode, absorbing as much information as possible. This results in having the ability to recall the traveling experience in minute detail. I can easily remember arriving to and departing all the places I lived as a child, in fact I clearly remember all the travels I've done throughout my life very well. I can't remember, however, what I wore last week to work.

This is the particular state of mind that feeds into one's creativity. It is a mixture of human survival instincts, because, of course, one wants to avoid getting killed or robbed or let alone get lost the moment one steps out of the airport. But more importantly, for the sake of creativity, this state of mind is nurtured by curiosity and desire. By voluntarily placing oneself in a new environment, to seek and experience something new and undiscovered is a natural facilitator of creative endeavors. An airplane ticket is in a sense a very expensive LSD trip with less chance of having a "bad trip."

Another way of looking at how mobility feeds creativity is in the act of problem solving. It is now common knowledge that the best ideas come when one is outside of his or her own habitual elements. You rarely get the floating light bulb effect (*the aha! moment*) when brushing your teeth before going to work in the morning. Has it ever happened that you're pounding away at a problem or obstacle with no headway? Everything that you churn up results in a dead-end, and you're nearing your wit's end. At some point you let it rest, go for a walk, or to the kitchen for a snack, or better yet, have a conversation with someone about an entirely different subject, and then bingo! Your solution is right there, popped right out of your head and you run back to your problem with renewed enthusiasm and desire. By pulling oneself out of that regular well-known place, even for a short moment, is what often will trigger a newfound path. This phenomenon can be observed among many artists, musicians, and writers who purposely take the time to be in a different place to nurture their creativity. It could be on the other side of the planet, or simply down a street in your neighborhood that you never walked through before; the importance is that it is a completely different place.

The point to note here is distance, a variable that is different for everyone with respect to a nomadic lifestyle. Though I have resided in only one city for the last decade, it is clear to me that I still live an itinerant lifestyle. At this rate, I could move for an additional decade throughout the same city before placing my furniture back in a place it's been before. I've managed to have very little furniture in the last few years because of this. I wonder if global nomad lady had a statistic for the *difficulty to hold on to things*. Despite this, I have no qualms with not continuing in the cross-global voyages of my youth simply because I'm moving just as much in this one place. The emphasis behind roving in a more defined surface area is that frontiers and boundaries are becoming more personalized, as opposed to the official ones that are imposed on all of us.

To clarify my point, I bring to light a small illustration I made before moving to the city, as part of a daily drawing exercise I committed to—filling up a whole book. The illustration is a simple outline of shoe prints with the words TEMPORARY TERRITORIES written below. At that time I was traveling on short trips regularly and the 200-page sketchbook filled up relatively quickly. I had made this little drawing to prove that borders, the ones we need a passport to cross, were pointless and unnecessary. Years later, while I'm, in some form, still beholden to that opinion, it is apparent that the notion of borders is one that, as a society, we will never part with. The surface of those two footprints proves this; the borders are still there and will always be. The difference is that they will eventually change or move. Even geographical frontiers, the ones that move the slowest, will eventually be modified, this can be witnessed today with melting ice-caps, deforestation, and drying seas. Borders are just as nomadic as we are.

While the concept of borders is here to stay, it would be safe to say that the nomadic lifestyle somehow causes them to evaporate, or at least become less important. I observe this often with visiting artists who come to the city. Those crossing Customs and Border Patrol at JFK airport for the first time often recount the traumatic experience as the border agent looks at their passport for an awkwardly long time, and they answer questions with sweaty palms. Granted, this is also brought on by current world events and security issues that come with them, resulting in a system engineered to control the flow of traffic. But for those who regularly cross these imposed lines, borders are dealt with like the safety bumps in front of public schools, you have to slow down for the sake of everyone involved, but you don't make a full stop. As opposed to impeding barriers, borders become indicators notifying one where they are leaving from and going to; a sign on a highway.

While the effects of this lifestyle are positive within the artistic world, and creative migrants have more expansive notions of boundaries and frontiers, the story does not stop there. This is what this strange speaker lady inherently communicated to a group of prepubescent unknowing global nomads twenty years ago. The act of nomad-ism is one of perpetual motion, designated to continue onwards. We are cursed to roam the lands, but in a good way.

Sebastien Sanz Santamaria has been living and working in New York City since 2001. He has been closely involved with the artist-run organization and arts collective Flux Factory, working in both the development of its programs as well as creatively through collaborations at institutions such as the Queens Museum of Arts and the New Museum. For five years he was Assistant Director of the International Residency Program at Location One. In 2009, together with Nathalie Angles, he co-founded Residency Unlimited as an artist-centered organization dedicated to producing customized artist residency structures to support the creation, presentation, and dissemination of contemporary art. After completing a preparatory year at the Academie Julien (ESAG) in 1997, he received a BFA from the Ecole de Beaux-Arts de Montpellier District in Montpellier, France (EBAMDA).